SPOKEN ENGLISH
ILLUMINATED

G000138883

WEST SUSSEX INSTITUTE OF
HIGHER EDUCATION LIBRARY

WS 2064615 1

AUTHOR
WILKINSON

AC

TITLE
SPOKEN

CLASS No.
372.6

Open University Press

English, Language, and Education series

General Editor: Anthony Adams

Lecturer in Education, University of Cambridge

This series is concerned with all aspects of language in education from the primary school to the tertiary sector. Its authors are experienced educators who examine both principles and practice of English subject teaching and language across the curriculum in the context of current educational and societal developments.

TITLES IN THE SERIES

SPOKEN ENGLISH ILLUMINATED

Andrew Wilkinson, Alan Davies and Deborah Berrill

With contributions by Geoffrey Robinson, Dianne Paskin and Gill Shea

W. SUSSEX INSTITUTE
OF
HIGHER EDUCATION
LIBRARY

Open University Press
Milton Keynes · Philadelphia

Open University Press
Celtic Court
22 Ballmoor
Buckingham
MK18 1XW

and
1900 Frost Road, Suite 101
Bristol, PA 19007, USA

First Published 1990

Copyright © The Authors 1990

All rights reserved. No part of this publication may be
reproduced, stored in a retrieval system or transmitted in
any form or by any means, without written permission from the
publisher.

British Library Cataloguing in Publication Data

Wilkinson, Andrew
  Spoken English Illuminated.—(English, language and
  education series)
  1. Spoken English language
  I. Title   II. Davies, Alan   III. Berrill, Deborah   III.
  Series
  428.3

  ISBN 0 335 09349 3

Library of Congress Cataloging-in-Publication Number Available

Typeset by Rowland Phototypesetting Limited
Bury St Edmunds, Suffolk
Printed in Great Britain by Biddles Limited
Guildford and King's Lynn

Contents

General editor's introduction

The publication of this book marks an important anniversary. It is exactly twenty-five years since Andrew Wilkinson first published an Occasional Paper of the Educational Review (University of Birmingham) under the title, *Spoken English*. His own present introduction gives something of the history of this publication and its successors, and the way in which Wilkinson and his associates came to coin the term 'oracy' on the analogy of 'literacy'. It is not given to many educators to introduce a new term into the language but 'oracy', greeted with suspicion at first as all neologisms, is now well established. (I recall being invited to a conference at Birmingham, which Andrew was organizing to launch the concept, and receiving the information sheet from my Head Teacher with the word 'oracy' circled in red and a note appended: 'Is it notifiable?'.) Now we have the National Oracy Project and a whole international literature on the ideas and practice of oracy, including the present author's *Oracy Matters* (MacLure *et al.*, Open University Press 1985) which grew directly out of the International Oracy Convention held at the University of East Anglia in 1984. Yet there is still much ground to be covered in the practice of oracy in schools as, amongst others, Pat Jones has shown in his contribution to this series, *Lipservice* (Open University Press 1988).

The present volume is to be seen, therefore, as part of a continuum, as part of the work that has been developed over the past twenty-five years, sparked off by the original publication of *Spoken English*, both by Wilkinson and his close associates in that book (most of whom return in this) and by other writers and researchers.

In addition it represents a continuum in itself in Wilkinson's evolution of his own ideas. The form of the book is highly unusual and original, combining as it does three inter-related texts. One of these consists of straight quotations from the original work; alongside this is the major component of the present book, the *Spoken English* of twenty-five years later. Finally, the third (and vital) component is a series of passages which provide narrative treatment of educational issues and ideas. (Students of inter-textuality should have great fun with all this!)

This experiment with form is typical of another side of Wilkinson's personality and career. I revealed in an earlier introduction (to Wilkinson's *The Quality of Writing*, 1986a) that his alter ego was that of Peter Gurney, the writer of experimental radio drama and winner of the Prix Italia. It is good to see a work of educational scholarship which is willing to explore new models of communication in this way, itself as newly revolutionary as the invention of 'oracy' in the mid-1960s. It is unlikely, in my view, that this will start a similar trend, as few educational writers have Wilkinson/Gurney's stylistic gifts – pity though it is that this should be the case. We are pleased, therefore, to be able to offer our readers two books here for the price of one: we hope that the narrative will be enjoyed and experienced as much as the more familiar educational writing, which does, however, perhaps unusually, offer an equal clarity and elegance.

The issues of oracy are paramount in the educational discussions of the present in the UK. The introduction of the General Certificate of Secondary Education (GCSE) established a place for spoken English as a compulsory element in the new examination, ultimately to be extended to other subjects besides English; the National Oracy Project is yet to present its findings and will give, presumably, a fresh boost to the practice of oracy in schools.

In England and Wales the issue has proved to be one of the major controversies in the establishment of a National Curriculum in English. When the first (interim) Report of the Cox Working Group on the English programme 5–11 was published (HMSO 1989), it was prefaced by some pages in which the then Secretary of State for Education and Science, Kenneth Baker, questioned the Working Group's wisdom in insisting on an equal weighting for the profile component of Speaking and Listening at age 11 alongside those of Writing and Reading. The implication was clear: speaking and listening was all right when we were very young, by the time we had come to years of discretion it was time to get down to the serious work of literacy instead. (The first page of Wilkinson's present introduction takes up this point in the context of 1965; it is surprising how the argument still has to be rehearsed in the political climate of education the late 1980s.)

Luckily, the wisdom of the Cox Working Group was supported by the National Curriculum Council (NCC) which backed the principle of equal weighting for each profile component and Cox stuck to its guns in its final Report (*English 5–16*, HMSO 1989), only compromising (some of us think unfortunately) at age 16 where they allocate only a 40 per cent weighting to the speaking and listening profile component. The debate over this is likely to be continuing when this book reaches publication.

What has been true in English has also been true in other curriculum areas. In general terms the work of Wilkinson and others, particularly Barnes, Britton and Rosen in *Language, the Learner and the School* (1971), has emphasized the primary role played by the spoken language in all learning – the whole philosophy that underlay the language across the curriculum movement of the 1970s was an emphasis upon the role of the spoken language; in specific terms no area of the curriculum has been transformed so much over the last twenty-five years as that of the teaching of modern languages with the emphasis that is now universally placed upon the primacy of communication and upon the spoken rather than the written word.

Recent classroom-based research by one of my own students at Cambridge – David Oxley, Head of English at Sheredes School, Hertfordshire – suggests that it is in modern languages and craft subjects that the greatest involvement in oracy may be found in many secondary schools. Curiously, there still seems to be much remaining to be done in the area of English teaching.

The other big change that seems to me to have taken place in our thinking about oracy in the last twenty-five years is the fact that it is now natural for us to link the processes of speaking and listening together as a single reciprocal activity. In 1965 we were still tending to separate them out; Wilkinson's team at Birmingham was, amongst other things, researching tests of listening comprehension. In the years after the Bullock Report and the setting up of the Assessment of Performance Unit, that Unit refused to seek tests of listening in isolation from other aspects of oracy. Cox has followed this sensible line by seeing, speaking and listening as integrally related elements of a single profile component.

It is significant that in the present text Wilkinson has (in Chapter 9) returned to the issue of assessment and seeks to provide a rationale for monitoring development in oracy that bears some resemblance to the models that he has already developed for writing development (see Wilkinson *et al.*, *Assessing Children's Language*, Oxford University Press 1980). The model for the assessment of oracy presented at the end of this chapter may enable more sensitive classroom evaluation of what is likely to be enshrined as an important element within the National Curriculum and, one hopes, an element not restricted to the English classroom alone.

To end this introduction on a personal note. . . . In 1988 I gave a keynote presentation to the national conference of the Canadian Council for the Teaching of English at St John's, Newfoundland. The title of my address was: 'Listening – a forgotten skill?'. Whilst I would defend the notion of the reciprocal nature of all speech acts, I do think that the active teaching of listening is one of the things least well done in our schools. Therefore, I welcome the brief concluding chapter of this book and trust that the outcomes of the National Oracy Project will give us further insights into how we can teach pupils to be active rather than just passive listeners if, indeed, we succeed in doing that.

Spoken English (1965) gave us an agenda for twenty-five years. *Spoken English Illuminated* (1990) is a progress report, and one that shows much progress has been made. It sets an agenda for the next twenty-five years to come.

Anthony Adams

Acknowledgements

Spoken English (1965), to which the present book is the successor, arose in the course of a research project at the University of Birmingham School of Education funded by the Schools Council. I should like to record my indebtedness to my colleagues on that first oracy research team: Alan Davies (also an author of the present book), Dorothy Atkinson, and Jean Price, the research assistant. I should like to thank as well Leslie Stratta and Peter Dudley, their successors, on the second research team, some of whose work is also drawn on. The excellent research secretary throughout the whole period was Pauline Roberts. The whole-hearted support of Professor E. A. Peel as head of department was both important and inspirational.

The first publisher was *Educational Review* and the editors have been pleased for Open University Press to publish this very revised version. Acknowledgements are due to Oxford University Press for permission to use transcriptions from A. M. Wilkinson's *Language and Education* (1975) appearing on p. 13, pp. 27–8, pp. 42–4, pp. 46–7, pp. 128–9; to Pergamon Press for permission to reprint the poem by Gabriel Ocka 'Once Upon A Time' from *Poems from Africa* (1974) ed. Howard Sergeant, appearing on pp. 45–6; to Julia MacRae Books for permission to reprint a portion of *Gorilla* by Anthony Browne; and to Jonathan Cape Ltd. for permission to reprint paragraphs from *The Silver Sword* by Ian Serraillier.

I am grateful to the University of East Anglia for granting me study leave during the academic year 1988–89 in order to write this book. Masters degree students of the university, Geoffrey Robinson, Dianne Paskin and Gill Shea, have kindly contributed sections of their work. Thanks are also due to Les Greenwood of Woodlands Middle School, Bradwell, Great Yarmouth, UK, parts of whose science lesson are considered in Chapter 7; and to Ron Leeking, of Kawarth Heights Public School, Peterborough, Canada, whose pupils contribute the discussion on parents' authority in Chapter 14.

The other major contributor to the book is Deborah Berrill. I have worked with her over the last four years so that now it is often impossible to tell whose ideas are whose. She is to be welcomed both for herself and for the Canadian interest she brings in a field where concerns are increasingly international.

Most of all I should like to thank my daughter Catherine Isabel Victoria, who spoke so much of the book.

Andrew Wilkinson

1 Introduction: the concept of oracy – retrospect and prospect

ANDREW WILKINSON

Retrospect

'The spoken language in England has been shamefully neglected.' This was the opening sentence of the original edition of *Spoken English* (Wilkinson 1965, with Davies and Atkinson). At that time reading and writing (literacy) dominated the curriculum both as a means of learning and a method of discipline. A parallel term was needed to give equivalent status to talking and listening, hence 'oracy' was offered. The need for it is perhaps indicated in the general currency it now has. It appears, for instance, in the *Oxford English Dictionary* (wrongly defined) and in the *Cambridge Encyclopedia of Language* (correctly defined).

The ways we characterized 'oracy' at that time were as follows: that it was not a subject, but 'a condition of learning in all subjects'; that it was not merely a 'skill' but the essential instrument in the 'humanizing of the species'; that it was a fit object of educational knowledge or 'awareness'; that it arose as a natural response to circumstance, rather than being 'taught'; that it was essentially interrelated with literacy; and that it was susceptible of evaluation. That these features have more than historical significance may be indicated by their substantial recurrence in curriculum movements in Canada, Australia (Boomer 1983) and New Zealand, and in such projects as the National Oracy Project (UK), and the Peel (Ontario) project, 'Talk as a Medium for Learning and Change' (Thornley-Hall 1988). In the proposals for the UK national curriculum Attainment Target I is Speaking and Listening:

> Pupils should demonstrate their understanding of the spoken word and the capacity to express themselves effectively in a variety of speaking and listening activities matching style and response to audience and purpose.
>
> (NCC 1989: 24)

This definition is limited by having testing rather than educational ends in view. Oracy is so much more than performance. It is concerned with the growth of thinking and feeling and its giving and taking through speaking and listening in a variety of circumstances. But the importance of the Attainment Target lies not so much in its phrasing as in its status as a statement of national commitment to oracy.

The original research was carried on in the University of Birmingham School of Education. The Oracy Research Unit (as it came to be called) was funded by the Schools Council to construct tests of speaking (Skull and Wilkinson 1969; Wilkinson and Stratta 1969) and group tests of listening (Atkinson 1965; Wilkinson *et al*. 1974). Although they have been superseded today, they were at the time responding to pioneering briefs, and nothing remotely like them had been produced in the UK before. In fairness to the workers it is proper to point this out, since the tests have been patronized by a few linguists from the high ground of hindsight. This is on the intellectual level of blaming King Harold for not using machine-guns at the Battle of Hastings.

Although we had the privilege of giving oracy a name its current acceptance is due also to the work of several who had insights similar to or beyond ours. Michael Halliday is one such (he read *Spoken English* and generously welcomed 'oracy' by return of post in one of his famous postcards). Others are Douglas Barnes, James Britton, John Dixon, Joan Tough, Harold Rosen, John Sinclair and Malcolm Coulthard, Leslie Stratta and Gordon Wells. Equally one should mention a different sort of talent which works for institutional acceptance. Thus the origination and formulation of the National Oracy Project Proposal by Keith Kirby for the Schools Curriculum Development Committee, its support by Her Majesty's English Inspectorate led by Graham Frater, and its direction by John Johnson and his team, have resulted in the active involvement of over half the LEAs in the UK. It should be added that the National Project had been preceded by the (very early) ILEA Oracy Project (1971–7), directed by Rachael Farrar (Farrar and Richmond 1979) and by the Wiltshire Oracy Project (1985–90) directed by Alan Howe.

This present book, *Spoken English Illuminated*, has a title recalling its predecessor and uses extracts from the 1965 publication, but otherwise it is a completely different book. In 1965 almost anything we wrote had the virtue of novelty. Now there are twenty-five years of theory and practice to draw on. Our intention is not to rehearse this material but to gain strength from it in probing further. The word 'Illuminated' attempts to indicate this, but also refers to the style adopted in certain chapters where 'illuminative' is alternated with expository writing. Since this is an unusual if not unique approach a word of clarification is appropriate. Research is usually presented in an impersonal mode which marshals references, describes experimental data and draws conclusions. On the other hand the human context is missing: the sense of felt life which is present in the work of a novelist. Both modes have their virtues, and in places we have used them in complementary fashion. There are self-imposed conditions: that the linguistic data in the illuminated account are not fabricated, any more than those in the expository, and that the illuminative interpretations offered can be supported by research. These interpretations might seem to be subjective, but it is a debatable point whether the presentation of research findings can be truly objective anyway. Illuminative accounts are at least quite explicit about their personal authorship.

We were aware in the heady months preceding publication in 1965 that what we were saying had more than linguistic implications. The Crowther Report, *15–18* ('Crowther Report', 1959) had suggested the term numeracy along with literacy as the two qualities necessary in the educated person. We wrote

> That Crowther can offer those two terms only shows how academic are the assumptions we make in education; literacy relates [people] to books, literacy relates [people] to things; neither in the direct sense relates [people] to [people], which is one of the prime functions of speech.
>
> (Wilkinson 1965: 13)

For this and other reasons already indicated we offered the term oracy. Numeracy, oracy and literacy we called the NOL skills.

> NOL are to our age what the Three Rs were to the nineteenth century, fundamental objects of educational effort.
>
> (Wilkinson 1965: 14)

It is thus interesting to read in *A Framework for the Primary Curriculum* (1989) from the National Curriculum Council (UK), a list of five conditions under which the aims of the National Curriculum are most likely to be achieved, the first of which is when:

> Pupils are properly equipped with the basic tools of learning, where numeracy, literacy, and oracy are given highest priority by teachers and are soundly taught. These skills form the basis of a proper and rigorous education to the highest standards parents expect.
>
> (NCC 1989: 2)

In *Spoken English* we again referred to this premise, that these three attributes were of fundamental importance. We commented

> If this is so then it implies a reorientation in our educational practice which in places will need to be drastic.
>
> (Wilkinson 1965: 58)

And so it has proved.

Prospect

The second Cox Report, *English for Ages 5 to 16* (DES 1989), which is a set of proposals to the Secretary of State about English in the National Curriculum, incorporates much of the best in theory and practice over the last thirty years. It is in the spirit of the original *Spoken English* and other books in the liberal tradition of English teaching. It is likely to set the agenda for the UK for the next decade. Countries such as Canada will have similar preoccupations. The Report is concerned with reading and writing as well as speaking and listening, but we shall confine discussion to the last two.

Unfortunately the Committee has inherited from TGAT (the Task Group for Assessment & Testing, set up by Government) a linear model of development – the pupils mount ten 'levels' which can be measured. The Committee knows that this bizarre idea that pupils ascend childhood in a series of vertical jerks is not tenable – that development is recursive (it says so at 15.20, 14.5) – but it has to make the best of a bad job and attempt to define the 'levels'. However, the differences the Report indicates between them are as much terminological as actual. There seems very little distinction (except in word order) between 'Listen attentively and respond to stories and poems' (Level 1), and 'Listen attentively to stories and poems and talk about them' (Level 2). Or between 'Take an active part in group discussions . . .' (Level 7), and 'Take part in group discussions actively and critically . . .' (Level 8). And of course further problems arise when we consider levels prior to these. Cannot younger school-children then 'discuss actively'? Of course they can. Given the right circumstances so can pre-school-children (this book will display ample evidence of that).

What the Committee lacks – like most other people – is the criteria which will discriminate between these levels, criteria which not only are terminological, but also refer to observable features in the language performances of the children concerned. In our view no satisfactory set of criteria exists which has at once a sound and comprehensive theoretical basis, and yet which is simple enough to be internalized for the important business of judging the spoken language on the wing. We have attempted such a set of criteria (Chapter 12).

The Committee is very sensitive to the problem, and the need for training and for exemplars (DES 1989: 15.44). In Chapters 13 and 14 we have offered exemplars of various kinds – story-telling and giving directions (ages 7–11), group discussion (ages 7 and 11). As far as 'argument' is concerned, we discuss this at pre-school level (Chapter 4), at 15 and at 21 (Chapter 8). The method we have used is to examine in detail spoken transcriptions, which reveal the complexity of the material and its recursive movements, so that it is even more difficult to talk in simple terms about 'levels'.

The Kingman Report (DES 1988a) inquired into the teaching of English language. It recommended an emphasis on Standard English, which Cox (DES 1988b; 1989) follows up (though this is far less an issue than either Committee seems to think – it's been commonly taught under the name of 'good English' since your greatgrandad's time). We write on the issues in Chapter 11. Kingman also recommended a course language for all teachers (see Chapter 10 in this volume).

Cox recognizes the centrality of oracy, along with numeracy and literacy, in the curriculum (DES 1989: 15.3): as we said in *Spoken English*, it is a 'condition of learning in all subjects'. We examine its operation in science, language and literature (Chapter 6), in science and drama (Chapter 7), in social studies (Chapter 8). In all these situations the interaction of oracy and literacy is important. We pay particular attention to 'argument' which has been very much neglected in the conventional literature-based curriculum. This is not to say that we support Cox's over-simple division between 'social and transactional language', the latter only being the concern of the school (DES 1989: 15.9). A study of the evidence we offer throughout this book (see for instance Chapters 6 and 14) will show that this distinction cannot be maintained.

Kingman's recommendation that 'explicit' knowledge of language should be part of the education of all pupils was also a proposal in the original *Spoken English* (see p. 89) and we developed the idea in subsequent papers (see pp. 145–6). A good deal depends on what one means by 'knowledge' – some of Kingman's suggestions signpost the boneyard of abstract linguistics, while others with a sociolinguistic direction are completely acceptable. Our own proposals in *Spoken English* – that pupils should acquire an explicit knowledge of language – were supported by a rationale in terms of 'wider control and greater tolerance' (see p. 89) and the excitement of curiosity (see p. 145). Cox's proposals see language knowledge arising out the pupil's 'own linguistic competence' (DES 1989: 6.11) and emphasize the 'social significance of knowledge about language' (6.14). We describe a 'language lesson' of the sort which Cox would commend in Chapter 6. We ourselves are enthusiastic to further a language awareness which capitalizes critical listening (see Chapter 15), and reflecting on the spoken language (see Chapter 11).

Issues which Cox understandably does not much address are pre-school language, the language of the home, and a teaching methodology implicit in the development of oral work. These are topics in which we foresee growth. Pre-school language and the narrative traditions of the home must affect our children's performances, and yet we know very little about them – except the myths. It seems likely (see the evidence in our Chapters 2–5) that teachers underestimate what children can do pre-school (Wells, 1987). Cox's early levels of performance have been criticized as being too low for this reason.

We also address the matter of the method of teaching. The point we are making in Chapter 6 is that methodology is ultimately a statement about relationship and trust, in a context where the pupils have other lives as well as school lives. The point we make in Chapter 7 concerns the role of the teacher in group discussion where a balance has to be struck between withdrawal and intervention, and similar skills, which are not in the repertoire of the traditional class teacher. Further discussion and practical suggestions can be found in such books as Self (1987), Wade (1985), and Tarleton (1988).

In 1965 we were fortunate enough to draw up an agenda much of which is relevant today, and indeed is still in the future for some schools, educational systems and societies world wide. Fast transport and telecommunications are bringing us more and more into an oral world. Once we read letters from others, now we read their faces; once we read their messages, now we read their motives. Negotiation is the name of the game in politics, in business, in marriage, in other personal relationships. But negotiation is not manipulation: to ensure this needs developed skills in oracy. We should add that these skills will need to be in several languages. To be monolingual will be to be linguistically deprived. To that extent, at least, many pupils from ethnic minorities have a head-start over the native English population.

In the original 'Spoken English' we wrote: 'Oracy and democracy are closely related' (Wilkinson 1965: 59). The Kingman Report is quoted by Cox as follows:

> A democratic society needs people who have the linguistic abilities which will enable them to discuss, evaluate and make sense of what they are told, as well as to take effective action on the basis of their understanding. . . . Otherwise there can be no genuine participation, but only the imposition of the ideas of those who are linguistically capable.
>
> (DES 1989: 2.17)

Ultimately that is what oracy is about – about not being manipulated, about negotiating as equals, about standing up and speaking the truth as we see it.

PART ONE
The humanizing of the species

The development of the personality is inextricably bound up with the development of language. Language is the basic and essential instrument in the humanizing of the species; without it thought above very primitive levels is impossible. Language and man are in continual interaction; change the man in some way and you change the language he uses; change the language he uses and you change the man. On the one hand the process of growth through education and experience causes him to reach out for new language in which to understand and communicate. On the other hand this language contains new thoughts and shades of thought, new feeling and shades of feeling, which help to determine such growth. His ability to direct rather than to be directed by experience, his ability to establish human relationships, are intimately related to his capacity for language; the frustrations of the inarticulate go deep. And it must be borne in mind that 'language' in this context is overwhelmingly the *spoken* language; even in the (historically) rare literate societies such as our own this remains true. Without oracy human fulfilment is impossible; speech and personality are one.

(Wilkinson 1965: 40)

2 Our first great conversationalists

ANDREW WILKINSON

The welcome

Sarah lay amid the tumbled sheets, one arm casually thrown back, awake but at rest. No brow more untroubled, no eyes more serene. She was by common consent the loveliest creature since the beginning of the world.

By common consent amongst the women, that is. They poured down upon her sentences like, Oh aren't you a darling! Oh aren't you a sweetheart! Oh isn't she lovely! Oh isn't she GORGeous! And there is special way of saying 'gorgeous' which makes the first syllable big and pink and cloudy. They pointed out her features as though they were not such as were held in common with any other babies. Oh look at her little arms! Just look at her tiny nails! What a pretty little nose! Oh what strong legs. Oh what strong little legs!

On such occasions certain topics are obligatory. Whether she resembled her mother or her father – or another relative most, for instance. And usually firm positions are taken up, though sometimes compromise is possible – the chin could be agreed to be her mother's and her nose her father's (though not necessarily as it is now) for example. Again it is necessary to predict her future. Long fingers denote a pianist (though many pianists have short stubby fingers). And large dark eyes foreshadow a beauty which will break many hearts (the fact that many hearts are broken by small pale eyes goes unnoticed).

No women meeting Sarah were ever at a loss for words. Not so the men. They would grin sheepishly and perhaps manage, Oh yes she's lovely, in reply to a prompt from their wives. Even factual matters they were usually at home with – data about height and weight, for instance – they did not ask about. Perhaps they did not see the same baby as the women saw – a bald, wrinkled creature with a disconcerting, even accusing stare. The language you use in communicating to such an alien creature was not one they had learnt, the emotions that went with it were not those they easily felt. They looked embarrassed and hung back, feeling subjugated by all this femaleness. How relieved they were when the host said reassuringly male things like, Let's leave the women to talk babies – I've got some beer in the fridge, or tell me what to do about my roses (my, not our), or I've got the match on video.

All the women knew they had a way with babies, knew how to handle them ('he would come to me sooner than his own mother'). They all wished to nurse Sarah. Sarah had other views, and when lifted up would often protest with a long wail of infinite sadness. To be grabbed suddenly by a giantess, strongly smelling of difference, with iron breasts not oozing nectar, trying to thunder gently. The friend would toss her up high and then clasp her to her bosom with a hug and Sarah would give out a cry such as would shiver the stars. To be whirled through the air as a preliminary to being hurled down into an infinite abyss!

Laura, Sarah's mother, was secretly anxious when Sarah was lifted up, and was unconsciously pleased when she shouted, and when she quietened on being returned to her. Relief. Home. I was inside and now I am sadly outside my home. But this is home. It smells of home. It is soft and deep and warm. A melody plays to me with which I join with gurgles: I sing the words to that tune. Until my mouth takes other shapes. My lips move for the taste of home. Feed me till I want no more.

The lady was humiliated, but did not show it, except in a slightly fixed smile, and in the kiss of farewell. The child (not 'Sarah', but 'the child') was obviously spoilt. She had had children AND grandchildren: she should know. But of course it was not her place to say so. At least not to the child's mother.

Some of the men quietly liked Sarah. Had she been their own, or had they been alone, they would have found a way to talk to her. Perhaps the sheer strength and certainty and gentleness with which they held her, would have spoken to her. Perhaps their deeper voices, though saying less, would have convinced her they were her champions and she would have been still. They knew one day she would be queen of the whole world and would have liked to have been her subjects. But how could you make a public performance like the women did? Perhaps in other countries – perhaps foreigners could. But they couldn't possibly. How could they! Be reasonable.

When the guests were gone Laura said to Sarah, How's mummy's little girl now? All right are you? Yes you are. Of course you are. You hungry my treasure? Yes you are. Laura need not have replied for Sarah, because Sarah kept replying by clenching her fist and chewing it vigorously, which of course means Hungry! I'm absolutely ravenous!

Sarah fastened on the proffered breast and drew with amazing energy. Laura felt the sucking on her breast and in her womb, and grew more contented. Sarah's eyes never left hers, and Laura poured words over her. Oh my treasure, my darling. Just a minute. Have a rest. You're going to choke. Let me wipe your mouth. Oh my little chick. My cherub. My little chicabiddy. And (one she had got from an old book) Oh my mouse.

When Laura had found herself pregnant she was not sure how she felt. Amidst the chorus of congratulations she alone seemed to have doubts. Can you cope with another life, isn't one enough? And as she swelled she began to regret her lost shapeliness, and resent what he had done to her, and he so unchanged, so invulnerable. The baby was born and the cry of birth gave her relief but no joy: she felt nothing – only sick and dispirited. There's nothing quite like it, she had heard other women say, and she agreed ironically with them in her head.

And it was Sarah who said Mum I love you, I need you as you need me. I listen for your coming. I calm you because you calm me. Wrap yourself round me and I am safe, and you are safe. My eyes seek your face. You are my universe. I dance my legs to your voice. Dance to you baby my little lovey. And Laura found herself echoing Dance to your mummy my little lovey. It was Sarah who said welcome, said it first. Laura was glad she had conceived and forgave her husband, and felt guilty that she felt she needed to do so. She felt guilty about her early indifference to Sarah, though Sarah had not been 'Sarah' then. Sarah however said we have always been inseparable. What is there to forgive? And Laura wept with joy and poured silver cascades of words over her head.

Sarah listened to all these words, all these phrases, all these sentences, as we would listen to melodies whose words we do not know or do not understand. So that the tunes got into her head and haunted it. At other times she heard other voices – in the house, in the street, in the shops. They were like a court orchestra playing in the background of her life. Some of the instruments she recognised – the harp of her mother's voice, the cello of her father's. Some others distressed her – the voice of the vacuum cleaner, the braying trumpet of a neighbour, the wheedling adenoidal fiddle she later knew as her grandmother. (That child is spoilt, but of course I don't say anything, never interfere.)

And if Sarah could ask in need she could also smile in pleasure. Laura detected her smiling, and smiled back at her ecstatically. And kept smiling broadly hoping to elicit other smiles. And sometimes this happened. Her husband made the customary teasing remark that Sarah's grimaces were just wind. But Laura's biting reply, Nonsense, do you smile when you've got wind? he found it impossible to answer. He did discover however that if you put out your tongue at Sarah she would do the same, with more certainty than she would smile. This annoyed Laura intensely.

Similarly Laura detected her first words very early. As Sarah lay contented she would utter bubble and squeak noises. Or she would sing mm mm mm mm mm. She's saying Mum, Laura would say delightedly. Saying it but not meaning it, her husband would reply. You are spoiling it, said Laura, but really sadly agreed with him. At first this babble went on continually with only immense sighs for breath, but then when Laura would come to her she could pause and listen to her, and then babble again, so that the two of them were engaged in a duet.

As Sarah grew older, sitting in her chair, she would sometimes make long impassioned speeches in no recognisable language, banging a clenched fist, like a dictator at a rally after a coup d'état.

Babies, our first conversationalists

Babies are 'conversationalists' before ever they can use language. They don't just make noises which other people interpret (though this of course happens). They listen to other people, and respond to them, and make signals to which they expect responses. It is said that they are 'innately skilled in turn-taking' (Schaffer 1974: 16–18). 'They look attentive while we speak to them and wait for an appropriate hiatus before they in turn make some gesture or vocal or prevocal response' (Newson and Newson 1975: 441). The explanation may be, not that the infant is born with skill in turn-taking, but that the skill of the adult, particularly the mother, accounts for the alternating form of dialogue (Bremner 1984: 192–4).

Whatever the specific explanation for turn-taking it is clear that babies are born with certain features which enable them to relate to other people; in Trevarthen's view they show 'subjectivity', the ability to act purposefully, and 'intersubjectivity', the ability to adjust their acts to take into account other people's intentions (Trevarthen 1969: 322).

Two important features of this social behaviour are smiling and eye contact. It seems they have an innate preference for the human voice (rather than, say, the voice of the vacuum cleaner, or an elephant) and will select it from other noises which do not resemble speech. And in fact they will move their limbs in rhythm with human speech. Such movements might seem random, but slowed-down film demonstrates this is not the case (Condon and Sander 1974). Again they have a preference for the human face as distinct from other shapes, and they seek out the eyes so as to make eye contact.

Such features enable babies to accommodate to the human world. In Mali a baby is described as a 'kontu', a 'thing', which has not yet become a 'montu', a 'person'. This exposes the difference we perceive between the bundles of instincts and needs which are new-born children, and the rational talking beings they later become. It is said that the role of those surrounding the new-born is to confer humanity upon them, and we can see the sense in which it is true as long as we remember that they have human potential from the start – however much you mothered a baby chimpanzee, and tried to take turns with it, it would be unlikely to become human.

What is conferred upon children is a human identity, and a social personality. They are told through permissions and prohibitions, through words and actions, what is expected. In this process of 'primary socialization' the children have no choice; they must accept the identities as they are given, for they have no alternatives; they must imitate and placate those around them because there are no others available to them. Not only are these the only people, but this is the only world the children have. It is a world in which, if they are fortunate, 'everything is all right' and thus is likely to retain its special sense of security and reality throughout life.

> It remains the 'home world' however far one may travel in later life into regions where one does not feel at home at all.
>
> (Berger and Luckman 1967: 155)

With the mother as the mature, most knowledgeable partner it is easy to fall into thinking that conferment is all one way. But this is far from being the case – there is a constant giving and receiving on both sides. Most of all babies confer motherhood. As Wills (1977) points out, devotion is not automatic. The responses, looks and smiles reinforce the feeling of being valued, and prompt the growth of love. The mothers of blind or deaf babies, because of their apparent unresponsiveness, may find more difficulty in offering warmth.

Again in language learning it might seem that all conferment is from the adult. But in one sense it is the baby who is causing the adult to behave in a certain way, for instance in the production of baby talk or 'motherese'. When adults talk to babies they commonly speak more loudly and more simply, with much more warmth in their voices. They repeat words and phrases, and use well-formed sentences. They ask many questions and frequently answer them. The babies are prompting this style of talk by their own communicative inadequacies. The babies' eyes are significant here. They blink very little, offering an uncompromising stare. Adults used to constant signals from the eyes of others seem to redouble their efforts to produce a response by some of the features just mentioned. Often they produce exaggerated smiles and grimaces for the same reason. 'Fatherese' seems to have a good deal in common with 'motherese' but for a variety of reasons – work, male role assumptions, and so on – they are much less likely to chat with babies, or to understand their vocalizations (Crystal 1986: 54). In the earlier years it seems that the chief transmitters of language, and the chief sources of interaction, are female.

The interaction is a source of pleasure to both parties. In the following transcription Ben (6 weeks) has been carried into the living room for feeding. The range of language bestowed on him is remarkable.

> *Mother:* Where were you when the lights went out? (*song*). Heh, golly, yes, stay down there for one second (*bib is put on*). What have we got for Benjie Bear tonight? There we are (*baby begins to feed and notices, as usual, the black beam in the ceiling*). That's my friend beamy! Oh, you've been scratching your face again. Oh dear me.

The mother sings, exclaims, gives an instruction, asks a question the baby might have asked, refers to him in the third person, and alliteratively, as Benjie Bear, speaks his thoughts for him about the beam, using baby language. ('That's my friend beamy'), makes an adult observation about the scratch but in extremely pitying tones.

Later on the father is also involved.

> *Father:* Come on little fellah.
> *Mother:* But Daddy, we want to go to sleep, Benjie and I. Wake you up for a cuddle. Won't that be nice, won't that be nice?
> *Father:* Hallo, don't go to sleep, it's time for burpies. Come on, get it up, get it up. (*Father burps*) Just like that. What a face. This is my intelligent look. Yes it is. Are you going smiley? Have you got a smiley for us?

We note both mother and father have a similar language. Both speak for the child – 'we want to go to sleep', 'this is my intelligent look'. Both ask questions, instruct, repeat, use diminutives ('little fellah', 'burpies', 'smilies'), make direct comment.

The feed lasted fifty minutes and was relaxed with silences. During that time much language was poured over the baby. The changing of the diaper was verbalized – 'One leg, the other leg. It's kickeys time', as the baby's waking, 'Have you woken up?' Many comments were made 'What a lovely noise!' Some questions assumed Ben to be quite mature. 'Where are you going tonight? We will have to buy you a bicycle.' 'Are you going to tell us a story, sing us a song?' Emotions were offered to him. 'You feel better for that, don't you?' 'Are you so happy?' 'You may well look ashamed.' (Text in Wilkinson 1975: 206–8).

It is to be noted that much of the type of language used above does not normally occur in adult interchange – the verbalizing of events and feelings as they happen, for instance, or the speaking of both sides of a conversation by one of the parties to it. It is as though parents in general write a play about adult life with stage directions, production instructions about the feelings of the characters, and a script for the participants to perform. It seems to be part of the intersubjectivity of parents to complement that of their children.

3 Primary acts of mind

ANDREW WILKINSON

Narrative and argument

Writing in 1968 Barbara Hardy speaks of 'narrative as a primary act of mind':

> My argument is that narrative, like lyric or dance, is not to be regarded as an aesthetic invention used by artists to control, manipulate, and order experience, but as a primary act of mind transferred to art from life. . . . What concerns me here are the qualities which fictional narrative shares with that inner and outer story-telling that plays a major role in our sleeping and waking lives. For we dream in narrative, daydream in narrative, remember, anticipate, hope, despair, believe, doubt, plan, revise, criticise, construct, gossip, learn, hope and love, by narrative. In order really to live, we make up stories about ourselves and others, about the personal as well as the social past and future.
>
> (In Meek *et al.* 1977: 12–13)

Hardy's phrase is a powerful one and it has become justly well known. Even so we need to ask certain questions about it, not in any critical spirit, but to clarify what it does and does not mean.

First, does it make too comprehensive a claim? Does it seem to suggest a kaleidoscopic fantasy life to the exclusion of everything else? Can the reader of the present sentences be said to be 'learning' their content through narrative? Does the builder who 'constructs' a house do so by imagining he is the Third Little Pig, or does he do so by making plans on rational principles? In order 'really to live' do we 'make up stories about ourselves and others' or do we, for instance, count our cash and negotiate our mortgages? These questions serve to indicate that there may be other 'acts of mind' as well as the narrative.

Second, it may be that narrative is a primary act of mind, but is it *the* primary act of mind. If there are others what is their relationship to it? Certainly it is preceded developmentally by other acts. Infants before they can ever use narrative use association – in language learning they learn to associate a 'word' with a person, object or action – 'mum' for instance with their mothers. When they use a plural ('men', 'dogs') or a superordinate ('food') their act of mind is to make a classification. The conclusion we must come to that the phrase 'narrative as primary act of mind' assumes certain other prior operations can be performed, and applies when children seek to order their experience of the world in a more extended fashion.

Third, are there other acts of mind which come into operation at the same stage – that is when there is need for a more extended ordering of experience? Let us consider a motorist who breaks down on a lonely road. We might describe this as follows: the engine stops, the car rolls to a standstill and the driver puts on the brake. Now the driver fiddles about with the engine, and decides he can do nothing with it. His description of the event to the passenger might be: 'The damned thing refuses to go.' Eventually the car is towed to a garage, where the mechanic does not think highly of the driver's explanation. Instead he examines the engine and says: 'The petrol is not getting through to the carburettor – either you've got a blockage in your pipe, or the pump isn't working.'

In this short incident three acts of mind are manifested. In our description of the incident we use narrative, giving the events in chronological order. The driver uses a different act of mind, however, the magical: cars do not 'refuse' to go – its 'refusal' could in no way account for the breakdown. The mechanic's act of mind, however, is 'logical': he looks for rational explanations for the failure. We thus discern three acts of mind: the chronological, the magical, and the logical. All these acts of mind feature prominently in our shaping of the world around us.

The chronological is the basis for narrative and moves into it when some link develops between the parts which is more than temporal. For convenience we may distinguish between those stories which are internal, part of our thinking, and those which are external – which we tell to others, as family and friends, and some tell as story-tellers, novelists, dramatists, and so on. Certainly our culture lays a great emphasis on stories. From the early years children in many homes are told nursery rhymes and fairy tales, they are given bedtime stories, their early readers in school are usually narratives. Television and film contain many stories. The newspapers are full of them: journalists call their news items 'stories'.

The magical is also very common. It comes into use when we describe happenings which outrage reason such as Father Christmas's circling of the globe in one night, and his descent down chimneys far too narrow for his rotund frame, or his entry into houses without chimneys where doors are locked and barred. In contrast it comes grimly into operation when some evangelists, particularly in the USA, claim to cure before mass audiences on television sufferers from organic diseases, who publicly throw away their crutches and dance in frenzy on command, only to collapse out of view of the cameras where doctors desperately attempt to revive them. It is to be seen in the popular papers with the horoscope – what the stars foretell. It is heard frequently in our everyday conversation: 'We'll pay for this,' we say in a spell of good weather. 'It's always the last one,' we say after trying all the other keys on a bunch. Both these remarks imply that there is some malign force persecuting us, for which there can be little incontrovertible evidence. Magical thinking is not confined to specific events or individuals. Whole civilizations have been built on what many people would now call superstition. (In education we must distinguish between the magical thinking which masquerades as logic, and that 'willing suspension of disbelief' which enables us to create and enter worlds of imagination in literature and art.)

Logical thinking itself however is a different matter. Our modern world is built upon it – on a principle of demonstrable cause and effect. The internal combustion engine works because it has been observed that a mixture of gasoline and air ignited explodes with a force that can be used as a means of power, e.g. to drive the car wheels. There is cause and there is effect. In the decisions of our everyday lives we weigh the consequences of varying courses of action – 'If I buy a new car I shan't be able to afford a holiday'; 'I prefer Ms X's policies, but she can't win so do I vote for her as a gesture of support, or do I vote for Dr Y whose policies I like less, and who has at least a chance of defeating the detestable Mrs Z?'

There are a variety of activities – recording of evidence, explaining, persuading, classifying, arguing, etc. – which are non-narrative and which we relate together under the heading of 'argument'. Because 'argument' used in this sense is another important organizing principle for human experience, we may properly call it, along with narrative, 'a primary act of mind'.

The distinction between argument and narrative as 'acts of mind' or 'modes of thought' has been established for some years in, for instance, social anthropology, but its specifically educational aspects have been recently indicated by Wilkinson (1985) and a notable paper by Bruner (1986). Curriculum implications are explored in Andrews (1990).

Oral narrative

Children's early stories are often what Paramour (in Wilkinson 1986b) calls 'Prechronicles' – statements without temporal or causal connection; next as 'Chronicles' they list events without selection in time sequence. Then may come various forms of 'Story' – episodic, or with overall coherence provided by some principle such as cause and effect. A good deal of work has been done on oral stories, particularly by Labov and Waletsky (1967), Labov (1977) and Kernan (1977). They discern several elements in the stories they study, and make categories which answer questions listeners might want the answers to

1 Abstract: What was this about?
2 Orientation: Who/when/where/what situation?
3 Complicating Action: Then what happened?
4 Evaluation: Fending off. ('So what?')
5 Result or Resolution: What finally happened?
6 Coda: General comment, summing up, updating.

The evidence of these researchers is from black oral culture, but the features have more general application. Take the following joke heard on television.

Don't speak to me – I've had a nasty shock (Abstract)
You know my wife, don't you? Lovely woman (Orientation)
Well when I got home last night (Complicating Action)
I found she'd run off with the man next door (Evaluation – implied judgement)
And I can tell you, I miss him dreadfully (Resolution).

This Resolution has a feature of many jokes, and short stories in the classic mode by such writers as Maupassant, Maugham, and O. Henry – the ironic, bitter, humorous, or tragic twist at the end.

The stories just mentioned are of course written stories, and there are in fact other similarities between oral and written stories in addition to those listed above. In them we look for the 'disruption of the probable'. Ordinariness does not make a good story. It is when something out of the ordinary happens that we become interested.

Children get an idea of what a story is fairly early, and this seems to be because they have been influenced by so many written stories read aloud to them. At first however some of them make a clear distinction between a story and an event in real life. Here is Victoria at 4.6 telling about an incident at play-school.

A little girl called Bridget swallowed a bead up her nose, and it went inside here, and she was crying very loudly. And Stella she just went to Stella . . . and then they both went to Helen. And Helen had to take her to the doctors.
(What happened?)
Well that's all I have to tell.

This is a piece of straight chronology which seems to Victoria not to need a Resolution. However, when she is asked, within a few minutes, to talk about her Teddy she immediately takes this as a cue to key into a fictional world where different conventions apply – and the deliberate use of 'her story' indicates this. What follows is a mixture of fact and fiction. A large hole appeared in a main road in Norwich – due to the subsidence of ancient chalk-workings beneath, and a double-decker bus half disappeared into it, fortunately without any casualties. Apparently Teddy visits it:

(What about Teddy?)
Well, I can tell you her story, but I hope you can hear this. Teddy and I were walking to school.
Teddy said, 'What is that?'
And I said, 'That's where the bus was.'
'I can't see it.'
So I lift him up so that he could see and he said,
'Oh is that where the bus hole? What they're going to fill it with?'
'That.'
And we asked the man when it was going to be ready, and he said
'In ten weeks.'
So we came – it was ten weeks – and looked at the hole, but the sort of sand was still there (*i.e. the hole had been filled but the road surface has not been relaid*).

And we walked back to school, and the teacher said you're the first ones to . . . come here. There's no one here.

This narrative contains many of the marks of 'story' listed above. There is Orientation – the characters and the setting, with additional information about the origins of the hole; there is Complicating Action – about the filling in; there is a Resolution – it was filled in (almost) in ten weeks. And there is a Coda – the context of the trip to school, and what happened there, reinforced. Children – and adults – use many of the conventions of the written story in the anecdotes and illustrations they use in their ordinary conversations. (This is well illustrated by the family stories we discuss in Chapter 5.)

We often speak about the influence of the spoken on the written language, and as the spoken is prior to the written developmentally, it is natural that we should do so. But much of our spoken language derives from the written, particularly in literate homes. Vocabulary and language patterns are acquired by many children from their reading, or from what they have heard read to them.

There are many ways in which this happens, and here we have space for only one. As children listen to books read to them they very soon acquire the ability to 'read' those books aloud themselves. They turn over the pages, taking their cues about what is happening largely from the pictures, and can 'read aloud' the whole book, partly from memory, partly using their own words.

Let us take the opening of Anthony Browne's excellent *Gorilla*, and see how Victoria 'reads' it, at 3.11 and again at 4.11.

> Hannah loved Gorillas. She read books about Gorillas, she watched gorillas on television, and she drew pictures of gorillas. But she had never seen a real gorilla.
>
> Her father didn't have time to take her to see one at the zoo. He didn't have time for anything.
>
> He went to work every day before Hannah went to school, and in the evening he worked at home.
>
> When Hannah asked him a question he would say 'Not now, I'm busy, Maybe tomorrow.'
>
> But the next day he was always too busy. 'Not now. Maybe at the weekend,' he would say. But at the weekend he was always too tired.
>
> They never did anything together.

Victoria, 3.11:

> Hannah loved Gorillas. She read gorillas. She watched television of gorillas. And she draw pictures of gorillas. Next day she asked her father and he would say not then. In the evenings he went to work and worked at home. And he asked her, 'Not now'.

Much of Victoria's 'reading' here is almost verbatim, even using phrases she does not quite understand – 'In the evenings he went to work and worked at home'. Interestingly she uses the literary patterns of repetition in the first four sentences.

In the interval before this next 'reading' a year later the book has lost itself, so she has not had continuous exposure to it.

Victoria, 4.11:

> One fine day Hannah woke up and had her breakfast with her best monkey cereal
> when her Dad was reading the paper.
> 'Please can you take me to the zoo to see a monkey, please Dad?' she asked.
> 'Not now, maybe at the weekend.'
> But at the weekend he was always too busy. He went to work every day before she
> went to school. In the evening he worked at home. Hannah came into his room, and
> asked:
> 'Will you take me tomorrow?'
> 'Not now, maybe at the weekend.' But at the weekend he was too tired.

The influence of the original is clear in Victoria's account. On the other hand she
has imposed her own story form on it derived from other literature, as in the
orientation provided by the opening sentence. She also adds her own details such
as that of the breakfast cereal, and 'came into his room'. Another feature of her
own is that of interactive dialogue. The original gives only the father's words, but
she adds Hannah's also, doubtless because she is to some extent identifying with
her. What we have here then is two story models interacting. Victoria at 3.11 uses
the model of the original, but at 4.11 she does so in terms of another story form.
But she can use yet another form. Without 'reading' and referring to the book,
she can tell the story in ordinary spoken language:

> Hannah woke up and sat down for breakfast with her father and mother, and she
> asked him to take her to the zoo, but he said, 'Not now, I'm busy'.

Victoria thus has three forms of spoken language available to her to tell of the
gorilla, two of them provided by literature. She is not yet 5.

Oral argument

Forms of written argument and of oral argument do not interrelate so well as
those of oral and written story, partly because their form is so different. Both oral
and written stories are passages of continuous text. Spoken argument can often
be a series of short utterances by different people, bouncing to and fro the ball of
discussion. Written argument, on the other hand, is usually a passage of
continuous text, debating or explaining certain issues. The present book is in this
sense written argument.

There are differences between spoken and written argument. Because writers
have the opportunity of reflecting at leisure, their ideas may be more complex,
more fully considered and worked out. On the other hand the very act of writing
them down tends to finalize them. In discussion ideas can be held up for
inspection by oneself and others, offered experimentally, changed, withdrawn.
One essential difference between spoken and written argument is that with the
spoken at least two people are involved, so that at least two viewpoints are
potentially available.

We shall not develop these comparisons further here. The point we wish to make is that the argumentative skills develop very early, certainly parallel to, if not preceding, the narrative skills. It is still a common assumption that when they get to school, children should first of all learn to write narratives, and argumentative writing will develop later out of these, because they require more mature mental abilities. But as we have just seen, children assimilate the forms of narrative easily, because they are so heavily reinforced. A similar process does not go on with the forms of written argument, and this is a matter which certainly needs study. On the other hand (as the evidence of Chapter 4 demonstrates) young children are learning the skills of oral argument very early, and this is in itself convincing support for this kind of work in oracy throughout their school careers.

Signpost

In Chapter 4 we look at the argumentative skills of young children, and find them developing remarkably early. In Chapter 5 we look further at the narrative skills of young children, along with the narrative skills of other members of the family. The stories they all tell are part of their history, and the way they interpret and celebrate their lives.

4 Home-made argument

ANDREW WILKINSON

The appeal

If two people want the same thing what do they do? One might take it, the other might spinelessly (or judiciously) acquiesce. Or they might struggle violently for it – as in the eternal triangle which ceases to become either eternal or triangular when the man poisons his rival or the woman batters hers to death. And yet again they might smile and smile and yet be villainous, like politicians who manipulate their people and destroy their opponents. Or they can negotiate, persuade, barter to arrive at a mutually satisfying conclusion.

It was this last course that Janet followed. Amongst her friends it has to be admitted that this was not the preferred method. You went in with the stiletto and took what you wanted.

But Janet decided to negotiate.

The prize was certainly worth pursuing.

There was a room at her grandparents' whose contents were a family history of childhood – no toy ever seemed to have been thrown away. To play there was one of the joys of the visit. Janet and Cory entered this wonderful room with delight. Janet sized up the situation at once. If you are three and a half you are fully aware of the need to act decisively.

'Can I have the doll?' she asked, and then, since there were many dolls 'Can I have the soft-haired doll? Can I?'

Her cousin Cory, a year younger, was overwhelmed by the wealth on display and had not yet made a choice. Janet saw immediately the need to deflect her interest.

'Cory, do you want this pretty one, cause she has this hat? Want this pretty one look, she has flowers in her hat. Look that one, OK.'

At the same time, Janet, realizing the need to get as much as she could in return for this gesture, drew several small dolls towards her, and offered the 'pretty one' again.

'Look want me to give you this one, look.'

Unfortunately for Janet her devices had only served to draw Cory's attention to the 'soft-haired doll' and she replied firmly, indicating it, 'I want this pretty one'.

Never lacking in resource Janet picked up a large puce rabbit.

'Look bunny. Want that?'

The rabbit's fallen ears gave it a dejected look but Cory greeted it with enthusiasm 'Yeh'. Janet followed up rather too rapidly by claiming the coveted doll in exchange.

'OK, give me this one, the soft-haired one.'

Cory, agreed, 'OK', misunderstanding which doll was intended, but when Janet replied, 'Not this one, that one' she protested, 'No, it's mine'.

By this time Janet concluded that the gentle approach was not working, and tougher tactics were in order. She took back the rabbit.

'Oh, where's the bunny? Where's the bunny? OK. If you won't have one, none.'

But the threat was immediately changed to a concession – the rabbit was handed back graciously. 'OK you can have the bunny'. And this was followed by an appeal to a principle of fairness. 'There, 'cause you have a soft one, so I have to have a soft one. What one . . .' The logic of this ingenious process was to give Cory the rabbit which she had earlier declined, and obtain for Janet the much coveted soft-haired doll.

Cory lost interest in the encounter, and began to play with some of the other dolls, which she showed to Janet for approval. 'I got a little Daddy, look her pretty hair', Janet praised the doll. Whilst Cory felt happy with it she would be less likely to claim for the soft-haired doll.

'Oh that's pretty, Cory'.

And they continued a ritual of praise, where Cory would lead, and Janet would follow. That's pretty. Isn't it cute?

> Yes that's a cute little one, cute hair on it, look.
> Isn't it cute?
> Look at her, isn't she cute.
> Yes, I like her hair too.

Meanwhile Janet was holding to her face her prize and feeling its soft hair on her cheek.

Victories, however, sweet though they are, are sometimes short-lived. Nor is the race always to the strong. Soon it was bed-time for the dolls. As Janet said, 'It's time for their bed. Her to go to sleep' and when Cory said 'Wait, I got her, her hat' (for dolls may go to bed dressed in finery). Janet added 'Wait, I'll get her hairbrush too. Where did you put it?' But that sounded tactless so she revised it to 'Where did I put it?' Cory suggested that it was in the box, but Janet did not see it there. They continued searching until Janet cried, 'It's OK Cory I found two. I found it'.

'Where mine?' asked Cory, a little distressed, 'Where's my two?'

'I don't know. You have one. I'm not giving you mine,' replied Janet. She realized by the look on Cory's face that this was not acceptable, and so stated the matter as though it were cut in tablets of stone. 'Little babies aren't supposed to have two, but I am.'

But this time Cory was quite up to the challenge. 'I am 'posed' she replied firmly, in a tone which clearly stated, so that's the end of the matter. Thus demonstrating that a claim on divine authority is not the privilege of a single individual.

Conversation at 2 and 3

Conversations with young children developing language are largely led by adults, mothers in particular, who use them, by no means necessarily consciously, to teach language and to give information. In such conversations children often offer a mixture of monologue, not to any one in particular, and dialogue. Thus Edmund (1.7) sees the framed photograph of a dog, and says:

'Doggie, doggie, see them doggie, doggie, doggie.' The dialogue continues:

Adult: Who is it?
Edmund: Doggie, doggie.
Adult: It's not just a doggie, though – it's our doggie.
Edmund: Our doggie.
Adult: But what's her name?
Edmund: (*slightly embarrassed laugh*)
Adult: What's the name of the doggie?
Edmund: Name doggie.
Adult: It's Minna.
Edmund: It's Minna. What's that? (*hook on the back of the photograph*).
Adult: To hang it up by.
Edmund: By.

Edmund's language is largely at the imitative stage where he copies parts of what he hears without understanding them. But he displays several conversational abilities. He knows that turns have to be taken, he knows that one way of proceeding is to ask questions ('What's that?'): another way is to point out objects of interest ('See them doggie'). He expects answers to his questions, and expects to give answers. Thus his embarrassed laugh indicates he knows he should answer but can't. He can recognize a question without knowing its meaning. And finally, although the adult naturally leads most of the time, Edmund can also initiate items ('See them doggie'; 'What's that?')

In the dialogue between Cory (2.6) and Janet (3.6) there are considerable advances noticeable. One question is not whether these children take turns (they can do that from the earliest months) but how they know when to do so and the kinds of offerings which will further the conversation so that it does not dry up. Cory is speaking of a doll.

Janet: Look bunny. Want that?
Cory: Yeh.
Janet: OK, give me this one, the soft-haired one.
Cory: OK.
Janet: Not this one, that one.
Cory: (*now understanding which one*) No, it's mine.

Cory knows that a request requires a response, positive or negative. And she gives both. She knows that you can initiate topics, give information to elicit comment; that you can ask for further comment; that you can parallel or echo what your partner is saying.

Cory: I got a little Daddy, look her pretty hair.
Janet: Oh that's pretty, Cory.
Cory: That's pretty. Isn't it cute?
Janet: Yes that's a cute little one, cute hair on it, look.
Cory: Isn't it cute?

She knows that you can dispute a point by suggesting an alternative (not quoted above):

Janet: It's time for bed now Cory.
Cory: No it's time to go.

She knows you can dispute a point by a flat contradiction, your case being stronger if you appeal to a hidden authority.

Janet: (*With reference to hairbrushes*) Little babies aren't supposed to have two, but I am.
Cory: I am 'posed.

Janet's conversational abilities at a year older are understandably more developed. She talks more, giving all the longer utterances, takes the lead, organizes the conversation and thus the play. She has a sense of what might appeal to Cory to persuade her to relinquish her doll: appealing first to her fear of loss, then to the gratitude, and then to her sense of fairness.

Janet: Where's the bunny? OK. If you won't have one, none. OK you can have the bunny. There, 'cause you have a soft one, so I have to have a soft one'.

And she is capable of offering other types of reasons. On one occasion it is terms of sheer matter of fact, as when Cory says (not quoted above) 'It's time to go' and she replies: 'No it isn't tomorrow' (i.e. we go home tomorrow, not today). On another occasion there is the magnificent formulation of an eternal law to support her possession of the two brushes:

Janet: You have one. I'm not giving you mine. Little babies aren't supposed to have two, but I am.

Conflicts are common in children's play and the majority of them are over the possession of objects. They have been observed to be as many as eleven or twelve per hour in small nursery groups (Garvey 1984: 141). Adults come down heavily on physical violence as a way of solving the problem, emphasizing instead primitive rules about the rights of prior possession, sharing, taking turns, and are usually reasonably successful in verbalizing conflicts. In observing such conflicts between young children (2.10–5.7) Eisenberg and Garvey found the four most common outcomes were: compromise; conditional agreement; counter (an alternative plan); and reason – an explanation of a position to provoke under-standing or acceptance of it (Garvey 1984: 146–7). Janet is in some sense using the first three, though there are signs of the fourth in her use of evidence ('Little babies aren't supposed to have two'), however dubious.

The bloodletting

Edmund came into the kitchen with a forlorn look on his face. 'I've got nothing to do,' he said. This was an observation which his mother had trained herself not to hear, and she took a book through into the living room and placed it on a shelf. Edmund followed her and repeated his remark, his voice in a tearful notation. Since this too made no impression he lay on the floor, rolling backwards and forwards, and promoted the complaint to a wail. This it was not possible to ignore. 'I've played with you all morning. I'd now like to do some of my own things,' said his mother. Vacation from play school did have its drawbacks. 'Why don't you do some drawing?' 'I've done some drawing'. 'You've got hundreds of toys. Why don't you play with them?' 'They're all horrid.' Edmund's mother sighed. She made one last despairing suggestion. 'Why don't you ask Lois if she wants to come and play?' Lois lived next door, but the last time they had played together they had quarrelled and called one another 'silly' and 'horrid'. Greatly to her surprise Edmund agreed immediately.

Lois came in, much smaller (though only a couple of months younger than Edmund) neatly dressed as always, in a high-waisted sky-blue dress, white ribbons in her plaited hair. Edmund, big, tousled in jeans, said nothing but dashed ahead into the playroom. She followed and found him making brm brm noises as he propelled a car around the room. It was as though she did not exist.

Lois hesitated for a few seconds and then walked across to a pile of toys in the corner. She picked up a giraffe of the 'soft toy' kind by the neck, and said deferentially 'Can I have the giraffe?'

The effect on Edmund was instantaneous. He rushed across and took the animal.

'No, I'll have that,' he said in a deep giraffe voice, and proceeded to walk stiffly up and down, chanting 'Oh dah deh dah, doh doh doh' as though that were the sound the giraffe made when walking. Lois reached out for the teddy bear, but Edmund intervened and took it himself. 'I'll have that. I want the teddy bear.' He then rocked it in his arms, rhythmically half-singing 'Oh I'm going to sleep today'. The giraffe voice continued, but perhaps it was now a bear voice. 'Oh I'm going to sleep today.' Then seeing that Lois had lost interest in it he threw it down, saying with a laugh, 'Eeh, he fell in the house', a somewhat approximate description of what really happened.

Lois had signally failed to make any advance with the soft toys. After all when you kidnap a teddy bear you have its owner's most prized possession, comforter, confidante. Perhaps a lesser prize. Lois turned to a zoo tray with its animals, fences, trees and buildings higgledy piggledy, with pieces of jigsaw, bricks, time-expired playdoe there for good measure. 'Oh clear all this zoo out' she said, half to herself. She was not a girl who liked chaos.

Edmund, still a noisy teddy bear, did not hear her. She repeated: 'I'm going to clear this zoo up, I am'. And the last two words were quiet but insistent. She began on the task.

These also were Edmund's toys. She would have to be stopped. 'Oh don't, you'll have a mess,' he said.

It was here that the tide began to turn against Edmund. Lois said 'Pardon'.

Now by pardon you could mean you did not hear. Or you could mean you couldn't believe your ears. (If I tidy up how can I produce a mess!) Or you could be making somebody repeat something to give yourself a superior moment. At any rate Lois said, 'Pardon'.

It seemed to have a discouraging effect on Edmund, for he repeated 'You'll have a mess,' rather quietly and glibly, and turned hastily to what might seem a better reason – that the researcher who was coming to record their language would tidy up: 'Dr Wilkinson's got to do that', a statement for which there was no foundation, but one which momentarily subdued Lois with aura of adult authority. And she then made the mistake of banging against the microphone stand. Edmund seized this further chance with a loud prohibition, 'Don't touch the microphone.' He had regained considerable ground.

But it was his last good moment, and he was not allowed to enjoy it. Lois pushed in an apparently guileless 'Why?' 'Because you can't' he rapped back. But it was a circular reason, not a good one. And Lois knew it. Back she came gently with 'Why can't you?' Edmund, without a reason, had to make one up. 'Because it's Uncle Tom's' (Uncle Tom lived a few doors away).

That this was untrue Edmund knew very well. So did Lois. Back she came once more, soft but insistent. 'Why is it Uncle Tom's?' In other words, how can it be Uncle Tom's when we both know it belongs to Dr Wilkinson?

It was here that Edmund began to realize he was completely outclassed. He began to panic and spoke quickly, and it is appropriate to admire the facility with which he concocted an explanation. 'Because it stays here. He'll take it back to Uncle Tom's.' That is, the researcher has borrowed it, and leaves it here, but will return it to its rightful owner later. But under Lois's dubious eyes he abandoned this and began to tell the truth. 'It's Dr Wilkinson's . . .'. But then he was freed from this topic quickly as she touched another of his toys, a railway turntable, and he loudly forbade her to do so.

But he knew that she would require him to give a reason. That reason was certainly imaginative. 'Don't touch that,' he commanded. 'It's poisoned.'

Nothing deterred Lois came in once again with her 'butter wouldn't melt in my mouth' questions. 'What's poisoned?' and he had to repeat 'That turntable.' She gave him a chance to get off the hook. 'It isn't really?' But he wouldn't take it. 'It is really.'

She offered him one more way out. 'You can touch it sometimes, can't you?' But he didn't want it – or didn't see it. Anyway it was too late. She was whizzing the lines of the turntable round on the base with her finger. She had not the giraffe, nor the bear, but she had the toy that Edmund coveted most at the moment, and she had carried the battle right into the heart of enemy territory. The turntable made a whirring sound, a whirr, a dance of victory. But Edmund, not realizing the extent of his defeat, crowed in triumph, 'Eeh, eeh, you've got poison on your fingers.' (Extended text in Wilkinson 1975: 167–9)

Fortunately the arrival of Edmund's mother at that moment with juice and biscuits ended further bloodletting. She was glad that the children were playing so happily together, and grateful for the moments of peace that this gave her.

The consecutive text of the exchange follows:

Lois: Can I have the giraffe?
Edmund: (*deliberately funny voice*) No, I'll have that/oh dah deh dah doh doh/doh de

do doooh . . . I'll have that/I want the teddy bear/right/eh we're going to sleep today/oh oh I'm going to sleep today (*rhythmic*) eh eh fell in the house/I'm going to sleep today.

Lois: Oh clear all this zoo out.
Edmund: Bash.
Lois: I'm going to clear this zoo up, I am.
Edmund: Oh don't, you'll have a mess.
Lois: Pardon.
Edmund: You'll have a mess/Dr Wilkinson's got to do that/don't touch the microphone.
Lois: Why?
Edmund: Because you can't.
Lois: Why can't you?
Edmund: Because it's Uncle Tom's.
Lois: Why is it Uncle Tom's?
Edmund: Because it stays here/he'll take it back to Uncle Tom's/it's uncle/because it's Dr Wilkin's/it's Dr Wilkinson's/don't touch that/it's poisoned (*she touches railway turntable*).
Lois: What's poisoned?
Edmund: That turntable.
Lois: It isn't/really.
Edmund: It is/it is really.
Lois: You can touch it sometimes can't you? Going round fast isn't it?
Edmund: Eeh, eeh, you've got poison on your fingers. Don't make that noise because . . .

Children of 4

Children approaching 5 have often quite sophisticated conversational abilities. They know how to take turns, recognizing some of the take-over signals, they know about not interrupting, about listening to others, about sharing out the talk, so that each gets some satisfaction out of it, about returning to a point. They may clarify what is doubtful, perhaps by reformulation, or by questioning, they cope with situations which do not lead to immediate (or ultimate) consensus. They can support one another, use forms of politeness, please, and so on – though such intention may be in the tone of voice rather than explicit. Indeed things like leadership, warmth, hostility, supportiveness are as much in the voice as in the words.

Such social or interactive skills are part of conversational ability, and Lois displays several of them. She says very little but what she says is very much to the point. When she loses the first encounter she chooses another route, and goes indirectly to her objective of status in Edmund's territory. Her chief device is to challenge repeatedly anything Edmund says, either by causing him to repeat it ('Pardon', a skilled use of politeness), or by the use of questions, 'Why?' 'Why can't you?' 'Why is it Uncle Tom's?' 'It's not really?' 'You can touch it sometimes, can't you?' Edmund's style is quite different – the assumption of a loud persona with the giraffe's (or bear's) voice, and an imaginative interpretation of reality.

The other interesting aspect of the conversation is the type of thinking it displays. Both parties recognize a proposition has to be justified by reason – Lois is asking for explanations and Edmund is giving them. One is circular ('Because you can't'); another in terms of consequence ('You'll have a mess'); another assumes ownership has prior claims ('It's Uncle Tom's'). Two are imaginative – that the recorder has been borrowed from Uncle Tom, and that the turntable is poisoned. They just happen not to be true. Their logicality is not in question, only their validity.

Comment

A good deal of work has been carried out on the conversational skills of young children (e.g. Wells 1987; Garvey 1984; McTear 1985). A very large amount of language occurs in interaction with adults (see MacLure and French 1981; Wells and Montgomery 1981) and we have looked at the origins of this. In many ways, as a matter of adult conferment, this is supportive, non-conflictive language. It is significant that one of its instruments is the telling of stories, a co-operative shared activity. When children talk amongst themselves, however, the likelihood of conflict increases. They are individuals, not extensions of their parents, and this implies differences of viewpoint, and competition for space and possessions, as well as the need to co-operate. This is the ground for argument as a primary act of mind to manifest itself, where children begin to validate themselves by reason. And it is remarkable how early this emerges. Out of the mouths of babes and sucklings comes the proof.

5 Home-grown stories

ANDREW WILKINSON

A family lives by stories

Home is a place where stories are told. This is a fundamental definition of 'home' which is not in the dictionaries. A family lives by its stories. Without them it is without past and without future, without imagination, without vision, without aspiration. It is here, and it is now – but no more. Its greatest expedition is to the supermarket, its greatest discovery a special offer on detergent.

The stories are of many kinds. There are those which retrieve and construct the history of the family, and those which go back beyond it; there are stories which envisage the future – what we will do when. . . . There are stories of humorous, scurrilous, pathetic incidents, polished by constant retelling. There are garrulous, reiterant, obsessive stories. There are stories which originally belonged to other people which subtly pass into our own family history. There are stories which are retellings from books; there are stories read from books, fairy stories, nursery rhymes – but even in the most literate homes these do not constitute the majority of stories. There are stories made up to amuse children on a wet day, which once started continue week after week, even month after month, till their originators are heartily sick of them, though the children never tire. There are stories children themselves tell. Stories serve many functions, but we have only space here to look at three major ones – the shaping of the past, the interpretation of the present, and the transcending of the here-and-now by the imagination. The following stories are all recordings from families known to the writer. The first three are from a collection one family has made over a period of twenty-five years so making a record of memories, some of which go back over nearly a century.

Most of the stories which follow are from adults not children, but their relevance is plain, for children are the inheritors of such stories.

The shaping of the past

Much pleasure is given and received in families by reminiscences of older members. 'Tell me about when I was born, Mummy,' says the little girl. 'What was it like in the old days, grandad?' says his grandson ('old days' being any time before the immediate present). Not to have started with one's own birth, but to be part of a continuity, is important to all of us.

Betsy (84) remembers a childhood where the rare entertainment was provided by travelling showmen.

The performing bear

A dark-skinned man came with a bear, and the bear had a leather collar and an iron chain was attached to it, and he used to stand at the street corner. And the bear would dance whilst the master sang. After that the bear would sit up and beg while the master went round with a can for the copper. (*Was it always the same song?*) Oh, he only sang that, because the bear knew the rhythm of it, you see. (*Sings*) Tally ally ump, tally ump tahhay. You can see the bear rambling round can't you? It was no more a dance than fly, but it was a movement you see. And then the bear would sit up, and the man would come round. (*The only song he knew?*) It was the only dance tune he had when he came our way. But I was only a little girl. But I wouldn't have remembered the tune, but our Joe used to sing it, you see. He used to have me for a bear. And he used to have the stick of the broomstick, you know, and I used to be swirling round this, and he was tally ally umping me, you know.

The resonances of such a recording are quite overwhelming. This may be the only eyewitness account on tape of such a piece of history. It is almost certainly unique as a description of the children's game following from it. Betsy's grandchildren and great-grandchildren delighted to listen to the tape and play the performing bear to the same otherwise long-forgotten tune.

Ivor (67) was involved in the invasion of France in 1944. He did not tell this story often, since it still pained him, but occasionally over a meal with friends or older teenagers, when the conversation grew serious, he would do so. It was well-shaped and had obviously been told many times in his head.

The worst moment

We had to clear this wood of Germans. It was a lovely morning and the larks were singing and across a field there was a wood, and there were Germans there. Some of the platoon had to give covering fire while the rest of us crept down a hedgerow. When we got into the wood we went line abreast from cover to cover. It was suddenly dead quiet – our lads had stopped firing, and it was dead quiet in the wood – no birds, I remember that. I crept along a line of trees and came to a sort of gulley, and there was a German soldier. He hadn't seen me. His rifle was against a tree and he was having a pee. We'd gone in to shoot them. But I couldn't. He was only a young boy, and he was having a pee, and I couldn't shoot him. I tried to creep away but I made a

noise – a twig or something – and he heard me. He grabbed his rifle and was raising it
to his shoulder. It was then I shot him. I had my sten at the ready and I shot him. I'd
shot men before over a distance, feeling somehow justified – they were Nazis, or so I
believed. But not him. He was a kid having a pee behind a tree in a wood. That was
the worst moment of the war for me.

The role of such a story as this in family history is important. Ivor needs to tell it,
on the one hand, and it makes clear to the younger people that he is not just a
member of the 'older generation', but is a complex human being like themselves.
On the other is a statement on the depersonalizing and continuing effects of war,
of the involvement of the family in great events, in a war, which like few others,
could be said to be a crusade of 'good' against 'evil'.

Roger (36) is a notable amateur cricketer; his ability at the game and his
enthusiasm for it add piquancy to his tale. It is an incident he has not yet laid to
rest.

The needle match

I've always been fairly good at cricket – I was in the first eleven at school. There was
one match our school played every year which was a real needle match, a sort of local
derby. We'd won the trophy for two years and it was ours to keep if we won this time.
But we had to beat these rivals of ours, and they were pretty strong. And there was
this girl from another school. I only saw her once and I knew beyond any shadow of
doubt that she was the most fabulous girl that had ever existed since the dawn of time
– you know what you're like at that age. I knew that if I didn't succeed with her the
rest of my life would be meaningless. We exchanged notes through the sister of a
friend and eventually she agreed to meet me on Saturday afternoon. I wrote back
saying it was an important cricket match. She said it was then or never. I was
desperate and agreed. We were going for a walk on Bodley Moor. So I made an
excuse about the match, and went to meet her.

Two things followed. She didn't turn up. And the school lost the match. Not by
much. We made a good score, but our bowlers couldn't get the other side out. I was a
bowler, and it was my wicket. I would almost certainly have made all the difference.

I've sometimes bumped into the girl since – she's married now with children.
She's always very friendly. I don't suppose she remembers the incident at all. A
pleasant enough woman, but quite ordinary – by no means one you'd go overboard
for. I just wonder why I bothered.

One of the functions of this story in the family was to sum up so much of Roger's
character – romantic, decisive but without necessarily weighing the evidence. His
sister regarded it with affectionate amusement. Of course she was ordinary, she
would say, only you would expect Julie Christie (knowing his weakness for this
actress).

The interpretation of the present

The pressure of the present needs to be coped with constantly, and story is an
important way of doing this. An inevitably instant reaction to events – a personal

clash, a loss, a comic happening – often needs to be communicated, interpreted, distanced, or perhaps enjoyed. Wordsworth said that poetry was 'emotion recollected in tranquillity' but story is often formulated and told, long before tranquillity emerges, as an immediate therapy.

Thus Janet (29) is trying to deal with an event of the previous week which still stings her, and which is having an effect on relationships in her family.

The mother-in-law

I know I'm making her sound like the stage mother-in-law but she is. I mean she is the worst! When we were first married and we lived with them for a few months she wouldn't let me do anything for Mike. He wanted to use the washing machine to wash his own clothes, but she wouldn't hear of that. Said it was the wife's job. I agreed for the sake of peace. But when I came to do it she wouldn't leave me alone. Once I'd washed some shirts, and when I came in from work I found them all in the machine again. She said they weren't really clean.

Anyway they came to stay with us last week. I have to make it clear I was totally against it but Mike said they'd been very good to us, and we ought to keep the peace, and anyway she was his mother – that sort of thing. We invited some people in for a dinner to meet them, and she insisted on helping me to do the shopping, making me buy the most expensive things. 'You don't want to entertain on the cheap,' she said, 'if it's money you're worried about. I'll pay.' But when I got to the check-out she was in another part of the store.

I made her go out with Mike while I was doing the cooking. She was very reluctant to go. She only agreed if she could help with the serving up. But when I was serving she was sitting drinking sherry with the guests. Actually I didn't mind that a single bit.

The meal was a disaster. I burnt the soup in my panic, and I could hear her sniffing out loud as she tasted it. At one stage I saw her obtrusively wiping the rim of her glass with a napkin. She really was determined to treat me like dirt the whole time. The climax came when I was in the kitchen and she called out, 'Can you bring some more wine, dear? Norman's glass is empty.' 'He'll have to wait, unless you want to come and get it yourself,' I said. I couldn't help myself. Everyone went very quiet. Michael was furious with me afterwards. It should have been his job anyway. 'They won't ever come again,' he said. 'Good,' I said, 'Good, good, good, good'.

In marriage, as Berger and Kellner (1964: 23) point out, the marriage partner becomes, '*par excellence*, the nearest and most decisive inhabitant of the world. Indeed all other significant relationships have to be automatically reperceived and regrouped in accordance with his drastic shift'. This process is going on partly by means of the story Janet is telling and the interpretation she puts upon it. The attempt of the mother and her son to continue the old relationship has finally come to an end. For Janet the mother-in-law is a stereotype with whom it is no longer possible to negotiate. The story she tells is helping her to understand and justify what has happened.

In contrast Helen (10) is telling of a school incident with great enjoyment. She has not yet reached the age when the answer to all parents' questions like 'What happened at school today?' is 'Nothing', and she is prepared to share and celebrate with family and friends. The story is made the more delightful by the deep authoritarian voice she puts on for Mrs Biggs. Mrs Biggs's near-disloyalty to the headteacher, Mr Baggeley, by almost laughing, provides spice at the end.

The space monster

Mrs Biggs – that's our nature-study teacher – is very strict. She's tall and she's rather like a sergeant in charge of a barracks. The other day in class we were talking about the solar system and she was saying 'We don't know whether or whether not there are animals from outer space, like Martians, for example'. And then she drew on the board a creature from outer space. And one of the boys who was sitting by himself, called Keith Bromfield – he'd already been moved because he wasn't behaving himself – turned round to the girls behind him and said, 'An exact replica of Mr Baggeley, don't you think?' And of course the girls burst – they absolutely hooted with laughter – and Mrs Biggs of course wanted to know the joke. And she said 'What was the joke, Keith?' And Keith went decidedly red in the face and said – he told us the joke and then we all laughed. And then Mrs Biggs said, 'I don't find that at all funny.' And it was easy to tell that she probably, that she was finding it very funny, and very difficult to keep her laughter back.

The imaginative world

Children are far from being minor partners in the stories of the home world. They release the imagination, both their own and that of the adults. Adults enter imaginative worlds through reading, through television and drama, through fantasy, through planning for the future, through dreaming about the past. A few write or act themselves. But otherwise there are strict limits to what is overtly permissible. The poet William Blake said that spirits and angels dictated his poems to him. He used to make remarks like, 'The prophets Isaiah and Ezekiel dined with me, and I asked them' (Keynes 1956: 185). Many people thought him mad.

But the worlds children create are not suspect in that way. In their stories and in their play they give free rein to their imaginations, and adults may slip into these worlds with them without suspicion of insanity.

Let us take two examples, an imaginative story and the imaginative play of a 5-year-old. This story, told at home, seems to have its germ in a tale told at school, which was reported as 'I knew a man, his name was Egg. One day he swallowed seeds. Next week he was all covered with daffodils'. The home story starts with the idea of a daisy chain.

The rabbit adventure

When I was walking along that time thinking about that man I thought, 'Why don't I make a necklace and tie it all round myself.' I picked up some daisies and began to make a necklace, and I began to knit some clothes. And first I said a jumper and a vest of daisies, of crocuses. I began to knit an underskirt, and out of again crocuses. I began to knit a shirt, and out of daffodils I began to knit a jumper. And I said trousers, put daisies all round my trousers, and then I covered my feet with leaves. And for ears I got some long leaves long sticks and tied them on to my hair. Then I looked like a rabbit, and I started to go all round the town dressed up as a rabbit (*said with evident enjoyment*).

(*Did you meet anybody?*)

Yes, and they said 'Who's that then?'

Then a child said, 'Mr Rabbit, Mrs Rabbit, walking along.'

(*And did you greet people? Did you say hello?*)

Yes. I said, 'Would you like to dress up as a rabbit like me?' and they said, 'Yes, well . . .' (*doubtfully*).

I said, 'Just knit a uniform of crocuses, and for your ears sticks and tie them on to your hair when you get some. And then you can go round the town with me. Should I knit them for you? They'll be ready next day. Where I live is 8 Clarendon Road . . . You can collect them at one o'clock.'

(*So what did they say?*)

The end.

The child's imagination builds rapidly from a daisy chain to a full outfit of clothes, from flowers, from herself to a rabbit, from a thoughtful walk to a parade in town to display her finery, from solitariness to a leadership of other children in instructing them what to make, and eventually doing it for them, because they are uncertain. The story helps aspiration to wider roles with greater freedoms and initiatives – walking unsupervised, receiving public admiration, doing things for others rather than having them done for you. Sometimes such stories by children become part of the family legends.

Another form children's stories take is that of imaginative play:

The wicked Jonkinson

To look at him you would not imagine he was the source of so much wickedness. He was small with an expression of sweet girlish innocence, and limbs of languid uncoordination, not made for decisive action. His very name, Jonkinson, given him by Catherine, was reassuring, suggestive of sobriety, even stodginess. It is true that he kept bizarre company – an emu, a Dutch doll, a tigger and a snoopy, a raggity andy – but these were virtue itself compared with him. Perhaps he felt different – not only was he small but also he was pale and green, and perhaps they were prejudiced for this reason. But surely not! – what with a puce rabbit, a luminous orange wombat, and a deep blue shaggy dog, a green bear was nothing out of the ordinary.

At any rate he was the burden of Catherine's life – hard when you are only just turned 5. As she explained: 'He steals chocolate and he is very wicked and he makes me cross because he does NOT get up in the morning to go to school. When he goes to school I have to carry him and he's always late. And on the school bus he always wiggles and diggles and dances about and performs, but the other bears say SIT DOWN and because he does that he gets sent out of school.'

One morning Catherine tried to rouse Jonkinson with the usual lack of success so she reported it to her father.

I said, 'Jonkinson, get up, get up, get up, get up, get up, get up, get up, get up!' But he wouldn't. Snoring in bed! That's why I came to tell you.

Her father asked what Jonkinson had said. It was apparently: 'No I won't get up to go to school the same as you'. To which Catherine had replied, 'It's all very well, Jonkinson . . .' but had not continued in that tone without also offering an incentive. She herself could not take a bear to school without special permission but at the Bear School Jonkinson attended there would be no problems.

I said, 'That's all very well, Jonkinson, but you can take your teddy bear – it's not a proper school. I'm taking my teddy bear because I've got to – the teacher, Mrs Walker, told me to. But yours is a nursery school – it's all right to take yours.' And she ended with the empathetic, 'You'll feel much better if you take it'.

But still Jonkinson had not budged. That was why she had come to tell her father. 'What am I going to say to him?' he asked, apparently nonplussed by the mutiny. Catherine was clear about this: 'Well, you can tell him that Catherine had to wake you up, and please do what she says, or you'll get told off by your teacher if she rings up. So say that to him'. Catherine felt that the strengthening of her own position, and the threat of the teacher's anger would help. She warned her father that only by being really forceful would he get through to Jonkinson, and she recommended both the manner and tone of the reproof:

'Well you'll have to say it in a cross voice. If not he won't understand. Say, "Jonkinson, Catherine has told you to get up hundreds and hundreds of times, and you won't get up. Please do what she says, or you'll get told off by Mrs Walker or Miss Honey if she rings up". So say that. That's all.'

This advice also contained the additional threat of actually contacting the teacher at the Bear School, Miss Honey. It is not recorded what effect all this pressure had on the recalcitrant Jonkinson because Catherine had to leave for school herself. But in general his attitude did not improve. Apart from one or two occasions when he tried hard with his reading and even managed words like 'cat' and 'mat' as well as – for more complex reasons 'jumblies' – his progress was discouraging.

In a last effort to redeem him all the bears got together, the fit and the fat, and the walking wounded, as well as those like wombat and panda who had honorary status because they did not seem to fit anywhere else. They were led by the (slightly insufferable) white (whiter than white?) bear, Pola, who said, 'What are we going to do about Jonkinson? I don't know what we're going to do about that boy.' Eventually an external suggestion was adopted – that he should be excluded from the Teddy Bears' Picnic. ('If you go down to the woods today you'd better go in disguise . . .')

Unfortunately the measure did not work. As Catherine confided in her mother, 'You know what Jonkinson did. He went to the picnic in disguise, and ate all the picnic when the other bears weren't looking. So tell him off.'

Catherine's mother counselled forbearance. 'He's only little,' she said, 'he'll learn.' 'Yes,' said Catherine, very doubtfully, 'he'll learn.'

Stories in school

In the first Occasional Paper in Oracy Ben Haggerty of the Company of Story-Tellers is reported as saying:

The 'bottom rung' of the story-telling ladder consists of jokes, playground lore and 'little sayings' and the hierarchy then moves all the way up to epics, myths and tales of the gods. The top rungs however can only be reached by appreciating the lower – the family histories and little jokes.

(National Oracy Project 1988: 8)

He goes on to speak of a school – and there are of course others in the UK and North America – where the range has been studied and presented:

In an Ipswich School groups of children studied different types of stories – family histories, stories from different cultures, Suffolk legends, dreams, and prepared presentations of their chosen genre. Ben mentioned in particular the achievements of a low ability group – the work was much better than anything else they had done, and there was a marked improvement in written work as well as talk.

(National Oracy Project 1988: 9)

Story is a thing everyone has, and is. In Old St Paul's, Balitmore, is a list or precepts dating from 1612, one of which reads:

Speak your truth quietly, and clearly; and listen to others, even the dull and ignorant; they too have their story.

PART TWO
A condition of learning

Oracy is not a 'subject' – it is a condition of learning in all subjects; it is not a 'frill' but a state of being in which the whole school must operate. It was argued in the Introduction that the NOL skills (numeracy, oracy, literacy) characterize the educated person; and that of these oracy is central. If this is so then it implies a reorientation in our educational practice which in places will need to be drastic. . . .

Since oracy is inextricably bound up with personality its encouragement is a matter of the fundamental attitude of the school towards its pupils; of their relationships with the staff; of the degree of responsibility accorded them; of the confidence they acquire. Oracy and democracy are closely related. If the regime is autocratic then the children are less likely to be orate than if it were more tolerant, and gave them a greater share in the running of the school. There are exceptions of course. In some independent and some preparatory schools, there is a high degree of oracy despite an autocratic system because the pupils possess a high degree of confidence and language experience from their home backgrounds. One finds similar schools where these conditions do not operate, and where there is a large degree of inoracy despite fastidious RP accents. There are a few schools where individual teaching is so enlightened that it can produce in the classroom conditions which do not operate in the rest of the school. But the general picture is clear. Where children are given responsibility they are placed in situations where it becomes important for them to communicate – to discuss, to negotiate, to converse – with their fellows, with the staff, with other adults. And of necessity they are likely to develop oral skills. This basically is how oracy grows: it is to be taught by the creation of many and varied circumstances to which both speech and listening are the natural responses.

The teacher–pupils dialogue is only one of those possible. Division of a form into groups each with a particular item for discussion, with particular plans to make or course of action to decide on, is a method capable of much greater application in most subjects than it has received. Some schools operate projects based on group assignments, which require discussion amongst themselves, the seeking out of information, not only from books but also from their families, inhabitants in the area, the representatives of business firms and public service bodies, from the local historians, librarians, newspaper, clergy, etc., involving the pupils in a large number of different speech situations.

The dramatic society is the traditional training ground for interpretative speech; but film societies whose members script and make films will necessarily talk a good deal in the process, and to a purpose; and a tape recording group might well produce original spoken material for entertainment or competition. Some schools encourage their pupils to undertake social service of some kind with old, sick or blind people, or to organize efforts for charity. Such exercises – quite apart from the other benefits – place the pupils in a variety of speech situations where communication is essential.

(Wilkinson 1965: 58–61)

6 Dr Jekyll, Ms Hyde, Mr Sherlock and Black-eyed Susan

ANDREW WILKINSON

The creation of circumstances

We wrote in the original *Spoken English* that oracy is to be taught 'by the creation of the many and varied circumstances to which both speech and listening are the natural response' (Wilkinson 1965: 59).

The art of teaching is the art of creating circumstances where learning can take place. The art of teaching oracy is the art of creating circumstances where talking and listening can take place. Both sets of circumstances are in good part co-extensive with each other.

A teacher is like an architect: both create circumstances for people. But unlike architects, who do not usually live in their monstrosities, teachers are essentially part of the circumstances they create. Architects work with inert materials which they bend to their own purposes, but teachers work with living souls who have purposes of their own. And for learning to succeed there must, for the time being at any rate, be a coincidence between the purposes of learners and teachers.

Thus Dr Jekyll, who taught in a county school. . . . But we are going too fast. Let us first of all meet Dr Jekyll, and two other teachers, Ms Hyde and Mr Sherlock, so that we can talk more knowledgeably about them.

Martin Jekyll

Dr Martin Jekyll obtained his Ph.D for research into the low-density culture of protoplasts. After ten years' work in a plant research institute on a series of renewable contracts he realized that the advancement he had hoped for was passing him by. Secretly he suspected that this might be his fault – he could no longer communicate with plants in the way that some people did; he decided that he was 'people oriented'. He took a job teaching biology and some 'hard science' in an independent school which was glad to get him. Despite a few Oxbridge MAs spuriously suggesting scholarship, staff qualifications were modest and a Ph.D looked good on the prospectus. He also was delighted. He had no training but an older member of staff offered him 'a few tips'; for the rest he depended on vague memories of how he was taught. He was determined to do the job well and soon displayed the energy and drive which had been less detectable by his superiors at the research institute. He made numerous mistakes, for instance teaching the wiring of plugs to pupils who had known how to do this from their cradles. But we all make mistakes. Although his quickfire manner somewhat bewildered his classes, the message that he was concerned that they should learn, and would help them all he could, got across. Today he was teaching the 11–12-year-olds. He planned his lessons meticulously. They always began with revision of the previous work:

'All right then. Can you please pay attention? You remember what happened when we burnt a candle under a bell jar. Well, what happened?'

There was a silence. The pupils were never quite sure what he wanted them to say. Eventually Jane gave an 'I will have a try' look.

'Well?' said Dr Jekyll.

'The water came up, sir.'

'Yes, but why did the water come up?' Jane looked a little downcast – that was not what she had been asked, and she felt somehow she had failed. However, she responded valiantly.

'Because – er – because there was a vacuum.'

But that apparently was not what was required either. She knew instantly from his expression. And of course from the words which followed:

'Yes, but why was there a vacuum?'

Jane secretly admired Dr Jekyll and it was a double hurt to be rejected when she had tried so hard. She gave up, in favour of Kenneth, who had had time to formulate something.

'Well, the candle kind of, kind of sucked the water up, sir.'

That was the best he could do. After all the water had risen up the jar – sort of 'sucked'. But Dr Jekyll's kindly amusement told him this was not right.

'How did it do that?'

He did not understand why it was not right, nor did the class on whom the joke was wasted. How were they to know that this kind of poetic language was not used in science? If you had said 'The flame sucked up the water' in a poem for Ms Hyde, the English teacher, she would have been over the moon. But not Dr Jekyll. He was still looking for the correct answer.

'Yes?'

Dan had been waiting. Science was one of his things. He had listened to the performances of his classmates, and now was sure he had got the right answer.

'Some of the air got burnt up.'

And it wasn't right. It still wasn't right.

'That's not right, is it?' he was told. As though he should have known it wasn't right before saying it. And meanwhile, Geoffrey, all eager, had been hissing, 'Sir, sir, sir' like an excited goose.

'Sir, sir, oxygen, sir'.

And Dan kicked himself. Geoffrey had the right answer, of course. That was what he'd meant by 'some of the air' but he hadn't said that. They awaited Dr Jekyll's welcome of Geoffrey's answer. It didn't come. Was it right or wasn't it? Dr Jekyll seemed to be chasing some hare of his own, to do with chemistry words.

'It was the inactive *air that was left, the oxygen that was used up. What's the oxygen called?'*

There was silence. Geoffrey thought, the oxygen's called oxygen. Dan thought, a gas. Kenneth thought, I'm completely confused.

'Come on!' urged Dr Jekyll. Again silence. He had to tell them. 'It's called the reactive *part isn't it?' (They should have known from yesterday!)*

To reinforce this, he asked Jane to repeat it. 'What's it called, Jane?'

'Reactive,' she echoed rather listlessly, not having recovered from her previous rejection. He followed this up: 'Why is it called reactive?'

There was silence again. Kenneth thought, He CAN'T want us to say 'because it reacts' can he? But that was exactly what he did want.

'It's called reactive because it reacts, isn't it?' said Dr Jekyll in a tone of some exasperation. The questioning went on for some minutes in a similar vein. At the end of it Dr Jekyll was discouraged. He had thought they had learnt a lot in yesterday's lesson, but now it appeared that virtually nothing had gone in. He would have to start all over again.

John Sherlock

John Sherlock had a degree in philosophy. Schools do not usually clamour for the teaching of philosophy, so he became one of the many people teaching English with no qualification to do so. He had little feeling for literature but the study of language appealed to him, and he taught 'language awareness' for some years before the Kingman Report told him to do so. The glib superficiality of the Report offended his analytic mind, and its irrelevance to the adolescents he taught depressed him. But by careful selective reading he could find in it support for the sort of work he did, and a defence against the good-humoured banter of the head of department for whom literature and life were indistinguishable.

The adolescents he taught in this rough Birmingham inner city school did not regard their time there as either interesting or worthwhile. The way to success lay through luck, football, or a record in the charts. But they tolerated John: he even thought one group, a small number of 14–15-year-olds with 'special needs', quite liked him; but their co-operation was certainly partly because he was under the particular protection of Terry ('You leave sir alone, sir's all right'). He did not understand why this was, but was grateful for it.

He had played them a radio interview with a miner from the north-east who had learnt that he might be well connected. They had listened carefully and had had no difficulty with the north-eastern pronunciation of the miner. He began by asking them:

'Now then, let's start by thinking what sort of people these are.'

Terry came in straight away, supporting his teacher:

'One's old, and the other young.'

Tony did not like Terry, being jealous of his leadership. He scoffed:

'Hark at brain box!'

To be accused of being an intellectual is no small insult, and Terry instantly turned on him.

'What's wrong with that?'

He snarled. Meanwhile Barry came in with a disagreement based on irrefutable evidence:

'He's not young – he's about 30.'

Mr Sherlock knew the rivalry between Terry and Tony, which looked as if – even now – it might result in violence. He came in with a more specific question, and was relieved to get a chorus of several voices:

'The interviewer.'

Quickly he followed this up.

'How do you know?'

A new contributor came in. Chris offered two sorts of evidence:

'He sounds it sir, and the old chap says he's 56.

The tension appeared to have eased, and he focused on his next point. The first had been voice as an indicator of age. The next was the regional base of accent in UK. But his question was too general for them, and after a pause he had to narrow it down:

'*What else about them? (Silence) Where do they come from?*'

Barry, always willing to help, volunteered:

'*Yorkshire, sir. The old chap comes from Yorkshire.*'

Barry had detected a northern tone without identifying the region correctly (though the pronunciation is quite distinctive). Tony, whose main intention throughout the lesson was to be negative, contradicted.

'*No he doesn't.*'

Now Tony was back in the discussion Terry was swift to attack him.

'*Yes, he does. My grandad comes from Yorkshire and he talks like that.*'

At least Terry offered (improbable) evidence, unlike Tony – and Tony was goaded into making a general statement in reply, which he probably did not believe:

'*You can't tell where they come from by how they talk.*'

Barry came in with evidence from his own experience to rebut this.

'*Yes you can. We went to my sister's in London and everybody said "You come from Birmingham don't you?"*'

He attempted to give the quotation in a cockney accent. Several of his classmates laughed.

Chris had been listening to the discussion and came in with an observation to resolve the matter. He took no part in the warfare, but appealed straight to the teacher.

'*Sir, sir, don't you change sir – if you live in different places you talk like them?*'

Terry pertinently objected:

'*Malcolm Webb used to live in Scotland, but he don't talk Scotch.*'

Mr Sherlock felt suddenly pleased. They were getting there. He ignored Tony's insult to Terry:

'*He talks brummie – like you.*'

All the boys spoke with a Birmingham ('brummie') accent, but to be accused of speaking with one they considered an affront.

The teacher ignored this insult (keep those two apart, he thought) and asked:

'*Are his parents Scots?*'

Terry said, somewhat mischievously,

'*I can't tell what his dad says – it's foreign like.*'

Anxious to elicit one main point Mr Sherlock asked:

'*How long have they lived in Aston?*'

Chris replied:

'*He went to th'infant school with me, sir.*'

Mr Sherlock could come to his formulating question:

'*So they've been here about ten years. Malcolm speaks brummie but his mum and dad don't. Why do you think that is?*'

He got the answer he had been seeking – the dominance of the peer group on pronunciation until adulthood is reached – though it was not quite couched in those terms. He was pleased, and stopped the discussion to play another tape, again followed by a discussion. To keep the inputs plentiful and the discussions fairly short was the method he found worked best in this class. There were only ten of them – perhaps he should try two groups. The trouble was that if you put Tony and Terry in the same group they quarrelled. If you put them separately they dominated the others, and the more thoughtful contributions of Chris and Barry were overwhelmed. Was this the sort of work to be doing with them? What indeed was? He'd have to give the matter a lot more thought.

Anna Hyde

Anna Hyde was head of English. A burst of activity after her marriage had broken down – a part-time Master's degree, and attendance at courses, two papers published in teachers' journals – had put her ahead of most other women professionally. She resented the way that she had come to this advancement (men could have both), while at the same time enjoying it – her power, her mobility, her growing reputation, above all her teaching. She had always been able to relate to children, especially to adolescents, particularly to the girls whom other colleagues found difficult.

One of the ways she did it was through poetry. A poem did not require you, or they, to reveal feelings directly. It was something outside either them or you, through which you could reveal just as little or just as much as you wished. You had to choose poems carefully. There were some – not enough but some – that were pure gold. She had always found Gabriel Okara's 'Once Upon A Time' such a one. The background was (she understood) of a Nigerian student's experiences in London. But she never explained this beforehand, feeling that this information might limit the response.

She read out the poem to the class who had the text in front of them. She read well – and knew it. Some of her colleagues would have wanted the pupils to take the poem for themselves from first reading. But Ms Hyde thought that when she read it you would be able to hear a pin drop.

And so it proved.

Once Upon A Time

Once upon a time, son,
they used to laugh with their hearts
and laugh with their eyes;
but now they only laugh with their teeth,
while their ice-block-cold eyes
search behind my shadow.

There was a time indeed
they used to shake hands with their hearts;
but now that's gone, son.
Now they shake hands without hearts
while their left hands search
my empty pockets.

'Feel at home', 'Come again',
they say, and when I come
again and feel
at home, once, twice,
there will be no thrice –
for then I find doors shut on me.

So I have learned many things, son
I have learned to wear many faces
like dresses – homeface,

officeface, streetface, hostface, cock-
tail face, with all their conforming smiles
like a fixed portrait smile.

And I have learned too
to laugh with only my teeth
and shake hands without my heart.
I have also learned to say, 'Goodbye',
when I mean 'Goodriddance';
to say 'Glad to meet you',
without being glad; and to say 'It's been
nice talking to you', after being bored.

But believe me, son.
I want to be what I used to be
when I was like you. I want
to unlearn all these muting things.
Most of all, I want to relearn
how to laugh, for my laugh in the mirror
shows only my teeth like a snake's bare fangs!

So show me, son,
how to laugh; show me how
I used to laugh and smile
once upon a time when I was like you.

Ms Hyde had seldom failed with this poem, even with the most unlikely class. Perhaps there is a nostalgia – a lament – for lost innocence in all of us which is moving beyond words. Now the class knew what to do – discuss in groups, and then one from each group would share their findings with another group. They knew also that later they would be asked to respond to the poem individually in any (well practically any) way they chose. Most would choose writing.

There was a hum of activity. The group containing Carol, Ian, Pauline, Sean and Susan started almost immediately on the meaning of various lines in the text – such as 'shake hands with their hearts' (l.8).

Ian: *It means, you know, shake with laughter.*
Pauline: *All hearty like.*
Carol: *Yes.*
Susan: *No, it doesn't. Not shaking like a jelly. It means, kind of, you mean it.*

Ian picked up 'shake' and connected it with 'heart' presumably having in mind the connotations of 'hearty', which Pauline also had – 'All hearty like', she said. Carol agreed, perhaps less from conviction than solidarity.

Perhaps it was by hearing these misapprehensions that Susan was enabled to formulate her own view clearly:

'No it doesn't. Not shaking like a jelly. It means, kind of, you mean it.'

And of course Susan got the point. They realized she was right, and there was a silence in which they scanned various other lines. Finally Pauline homed in on the fourth verse.

'I like that bit about faces. He says the faces are like dresses. You know you put a different dress on when you feel different.'

There was a sympathetic murmur from the girls, which alienated Ian.
'*I don't,*' *he said.*
He was completely (and deliberately) cold-shouldered by the girls. Carol said:
'*I put this one on to come to school and when I get home I can't wait to get out of it.*'
And Pauline added:
'*You feel a different person.*' *The girls at least were interpreting the poems in terms of their own experiences. But the topic was now changing direction as the girl-talk continued, with Susan's evaluative:*
'*If you have too many things it's showing off. Sally Turner even had a special dress for . . .*'
The ending was heard by the girls (or perhaps they knew it without the words being said), who dissolved in laughter. But not by the boys.
Ian resented his exclusion, and tried to get back into the conversation with the aggressive, '*What do you need a lot for? Waste of money.*' *Pauline took him on:*
'*Girls need more clothes than boys.*'
*Sean said very little throughout the whole subsequent discussion, but was prompted to come to the male defence: '*Why do they?*'
*Carol turned on him with scorn: '*Course they do, everybody knows that.*'
Ms Hyde moved over towards the group. They grinned and returned to the poem. This male–female debate was part of their life together in the class from which both sexes got a good deal of pleasure. It could be resumed at any time. They looked at various parts of the poem.
Later Carol returned to the lines about faces:
'*Homeface, you know, like this.*'
She was an excellent mimic, and gave herself a surly expression and hangdog shoulders. They enjoyed this and were eager to compete. Pauline came in with:
'*What about office face?*' *and made a prim-mouthed hoity face. But after the laughter had died Susan, who had not been taking part in the mimicry, said seriously:*
'*I like the next line, about a fixed portrait smile. You know when your photo has a silly grin on you didn't want.*'
They responded to this. That was in the experience of them all. And when you particularly wanted a good picture to impress a boy or a girl . . .
There was a pause. It was as though by offering her experience, Susan had empowered Ian to examine his. He said meditatively:
'*It's like when your face begins to ache when you try to keep up a smile for people, relatives, and that.*'
Anna Hyde was well pleased with the discussion so far, though with five groups it was difficult to monitor what was going on much of the time. But Susan's group (she unconsciously identified it by the liveliest person in it) seemed to be relating it to their own lives, even acting out bits of it. She would have more evidence when she could look at the subsequent work.

Black-eyed Susan

Susan came out from Anna Hyde's lesson. She had enjoyed the discussion – yes, she really had. Slight, dark-eyed and pallid from the challenge, she rehearsed in retrospect the argument about the equality of the sexes. Ian had been saying some silly things, she thought, and she'd kept asking why. Pushing him back, Why? Yes but why? He had said that God was male and she'd asked him how he knew. And anyway, she'd countered, there were religions in which God was female. She had not been sure which these were and so she was glad he did not have a chance to ask her before Sean, whose obsession was sport, rushed in with, 'Men can run faster than women'. It was Ian, grateful to escape from Susan's hammering, who turned on him with the scornful 'What does that matter? There's things more important than sport'. (Ian had academic aspirations.) Susan liked Ian. If the truth were known she was quite sweet on Ian. And now he was looking at her with respect from those oh so blue eyes. He was actually siding with her against this chauvinistic fanatic. She walked along behind a dazed smile. It really had been a good discussion in Ms Hyde's lesson. And of course there had been the poem as well. They had been brought back to that when Pauline had said. 'Look this isn't what we're. . . Let's get back to what we were supposed to be talking about.' Yes, the poem had been good: she'd liked the poem. Ms Hyde had said they'd got to make a response to it. In any way they wanted. For homework.

So that night she tried. She wrote a poem. It didn't take much time – it kind of flowed. There it was on the page. She believed in inspiration. Either it came, settling on the page like a beautiful butterfly, or it didn't. She hated drafting and revising – it always made it worse.

They're All Me

I have learnt to wear many faces,
Sad face, glad face, sulky face,
Pleasant face when I want something.

I have learnt to wear many faces,
Angry face, hating face, nasty face,
Pleading face when I want something

But I'm not really wearing them,
They're all me.

When she read it through she realized she had taken some lines from the original:
I have learnt to wear many faces.
So what? – the bit at the end was hers:
But I'm not really wearing them,
They're all me.
That was hers. She'd often thought you can't pretend to be what you're not. Her mother criticised people who gave themselves airs. She hoped Ms Hyde would like it. She had written it for Ms Hyde. She liked Ms Hyde. If you really had to grow old – and Ms Hyde must be at least 35 – it was better to be like her. Be nice, and don't get fat, and dress well. And don't pretend you are one of the kids, because you're NOT! Yes, she really hoped Ms Hyde would like it. She usually did.

Dr Jekyll, Ms Hyde and Mr Sherlock

Martin Jekyll, Anna Hyde and John Sherlock are real teachers, though those are not their real names, and the dialogues quoted are edited from their lessons. They are very different in background, personality and teaching style.

Martin Jekyll, teaching science, is playing the game of 'guess what's in my head'. This is a revision section of the lesson so it is quite permissible to seek for particular answers as a means of finding out what has been learnt. The difficulty is that Dr Jekyll is in effect testing, not whether they have understood the concepts, but whether they have learnt certain vocabulary. When Dan said 'some of the air' and Geoffrey said 'oxygen' it seems that they both had the concept. But the teacher did not respond to those items. He had a fixed agenda which prevented him from doing so. When Kenneth said 'The candle sucked up the water' he was using a metaphorical style of language which had no place in Martin Jekyll's view of the subject. Of course exact vocabulary is necessary for the study of science but the teacher's insistence on it at this stage prevented his exploring what degree of understanding his class possessed. At the end of the exchange he felt they had learnt very little, which seems manifestly untrue. Thus even on its own terms this revision technique was a failure. Dr Jekyll was comparatively inexperienced, but research (e.g. Barnes *et al.* 1971; Carré 1981) suggests experienced science teachers may lay undue weight on technical vocabulary.

Anna Hyde is a professional. She has experience which will enable her to give responsibility to her classes to learn for themselves. She has an unobtrusive overall control which allows them to develop – within limits – their own agenda. They have worked in groups before and have confidence in one another. She recognizes that there are apparent irrelevances in the course of a discussion which are in the psychological interests of people spending long periods together. This does not mean that there are not some forms of gossip leading away from the issues, and concerned not with challenge but with solidarity. Predominantly these boys and girls are using their own language to come to terms with the poem. She is not asking 'What do you feel?' but their feelings are emerging in terms of their own experiences.

Whereas Anna Hyde has no apparent problems of control – it has been established quietly over a period and does not need assertion – John Sherlock is in a school where control is constantly challenged. His teaching highlights language as both a learning and a control device. He does not feel able, at least at the present time, to relinquish control of the lesson to the degree that group work would demand. If you put Terry and Tony in the same group they would quarrel, he argues, reminding you that Terry is on probation. If you put them in separate ones they would dominate the others. So he makes as much use of their ideas as he feels he can, and builds his points upon them. This is anyway a common teaching technique, and he handles it well, treading carefully across the mine-field. It prompts the question whether each individual who contributes an item possesses at the end the total concept that is built up – or whether it is just in the teacher's mind. Do the bricks perceive the building? Nevertheless the technique is a useful one and much learning goes on by it, particularly when its discoveries are fed back. What it does not do is to give responsibility to the members of the class for their own learning. And it is responsibility for this that Terry and Tony lack.

Comment

We must create circumstances: in these the students develop their oracy and their literacy. But this is not easy. The language that Martin Jekyll elicited from his group was limited by his own sense of the nature and uses of language. That which John Sherlock obtained from his was restricted by his perceptions of a difficult class. Only Anna Hyde was able to produce a climate in which the ideas of her students began to bloom. And this is because ultimately, despite the caring of the other two, only Anna Hyde had faith in her students.

Anna Hyde was very pleased with Susan's poem. And Susan felt encouraged to think about – to feel about – another poem. Perhaps if she took a white sheet of paper and laid it out another brilliant butterfly would settle on it. She did not know what this poem would be about – yet. But one thing she was quite certain of. Whatever it was about it would not be about Ian. She certainly would not write a poem in which Ian figured – not even a poem upon which he had the slightest influence. Not in any way at all.

7 Across the curriculum

ANDREW WILKINSON with
DIANNE PASKIN

Oracy and literacy

The first edition of *Spoken English* (Wilkinson 1965) described oracy as 'a condition of learning in all subjects'. In 1971 the notable *Language, the Learner, and the School* (Barnes *et al.* 1971) advocated 'language across the curriculum', a concept given official support by the Bullock Report (1975). It seems that such statements were indicative of the way ideas were moving towards the recognition that we have today of the role of language in learning throughout the school.

Oracy and literacy are the texture of classroom activity. They are complementary, not competitive. They are not the same – talking about something is not the same as writing about it; hearing about it is not the same as reading about it; the thinking involved in both may be very different. Both make their contribution to our learning, hence work involving both maximizes their value.

A good example is the type of project involving a study of 'living history'. Many people in the UK have direct experience of the Second World War and hence a theme such as 'Life in Wartime' is one with plenty of rich testimony to draw on. Typically such a project may involve groups' specializing on a particular theme: schooling, supplies and transport, enemy action, the soldier's life, the role of women, and so on. In the course of such a project a whole range of different types of language activities will be involved. Groups plan their work, they read up the background, they interview and record older people in their families and the community. They have interim discussions on what they are learning, play and discuss some tapes. They consider their final reports – who should write what – and then write them. They plan for a final presentation to a wider group – the class, the year, parents and friends who have taken part. They make the presentation. The language in the project ranges from personal to public, from short turns to long turns, from written notes to written reports.

An example of a similar project was that carried out with upper juniors by Locking Stumps Primary School, Cheshire, on the theme 'Children at War '39–'45'. The teachers involved argued that long before history was written down it was passed from one generation to another through stories and songs about a community's past. They felt that they had a superb opportunity to capitalize on this. The children were very carefully prepared beforehand. They worked in groups learning the difference between open and closed questions, and the art of structuring questions for the best effect. The pupils worked in pairs in the school to practise their new skills and familiarize themselves with the technicalities of recording. The tapes they made became a great teaching resource. Some pupils shared their recorded talks with each other, while others went further, transcribing their favourite reminiscences and preparing a wall display with speech bubbles. The teachers considered that the most impressive outcome of the work was the energy and enthusiasm generated in the pupils. 'By taking responsibility for the interviews from early preparation through to successful completion, they developed a real sense of ownership for the project which greatly enhanced its results' (Harris 1989: 38).

This study is part of the Cheshire Oracy Project, one of the many going ahead under the auspices of the National Oracy Project (NOP) involving many local education authorities in the UK. One of the declared aims of the NOP is 'to improve pupil's performance across the curriculum'. The director, John Johnson, writes:

> Whether the subject matter is primary mathematics, or secondary history, whether it's science or technology, geography or social education, all those involved in the changes can point to a marked shift in the perception of the role talk should play; witness this one example from *Maths Talk*, a publication by the Mathematical Association (1987) which is devoted to ways of developing mathematics through talk:
> 'The skills of oral language are just as important in mathematics as they are in other aspects of the primary curriculum.'
>
> (Johnson 1988: 2)

An illustration may be taken from work at the Benson Primary School in the Croydon Oracy Project (Sokoloff 1989: 19). Four 10-year-olds are seeking to discover how many axes of symmetry there are in a variety of polygons:

K: I've found five on the first one.
E: So there must be more on the second one. It must be . . .
K: So there are six on here.
C: Yes, hold on. One, two, three, four.
K: There's got to be a pattern somewhere.
K: Yes, 'cos that's what most maths things do . . .
C: No I don't think we can get more than six.
E: 'Cos it's an even number.

Analysis, mutual support, prediction, the giving of reason, the possibility of a pattern, are contributions made in the spoken language to the thinking going on even in these few exchanges.

A concluding example comes from early science work at Havenwood Public School, Mississauga, as part of the Peel project, *Talk, a Medium for Learning and*

Change, sponsored by the Ontario Ministry of Education (Thornley-Hall 1988). Susan Huff put a problem to some of her Grade Three children (7–8 year olds), asking whether a marble would run further if the block of wood supporting the ruler it was to run down were higher. A few of the responses were:

Namje: Well Miss Huff, let's stop all the talk and get on with the experiment.
Kris: No, because the marble will move slower and shorter because it's like fat people – they have trouble moving. I'm sorry Nicole, I didn't mean to say that rude part about fat people. Actually Nicole you are a pretty good runner. I've changed my mind – I've decided that the marble will move faster if the block of wood is higher.
Steve: The marble will get stuck in the middle of the ruler because it looks like there is a piece of gum on the ruler.
Andrew: I bet I could come up with a better experiment. Like making dinosaurs lay eggs and race the eggs down the hill.

To study this is to learn much about the mental operations of young children. Here they could not on the whole think abstractly about the problem. Namje seemed to recognize this by requiring a demonstration. Steve looked at the experiment practically and found a good reason why it would come to nothing. Andrew replicated the form of the experiment in imaginative terms – with the dinosaurs' eggs – but offered nothing towards a solution. Kris, however, was really concerned to solve the problem. His first attempt – by analogy with fat people – was a non-sequitur. But then – even while he was apologizing to Nichole about his unintended insult – he seems to have had an inspiration and his second attempt was (if we equate 'further' with 'faster') the right answer.

It is not possible to discuss all the different kinds of learning going on in the range of situations in schools. The further sections of this chapter will instead look in some detail at activities in two areas – science and literature.

Problem-solving in science
Dianne Paskin

'Break up our mum's antiques?': the group at work.

Groups of mixed ability children, 12–13-year-olds, were asked to

Design an experiment to show why it is often necessary to have gaps built into railway lines at regular spacings. Would the type of metal affect the size of gaps needed?

The group recorded consists of Dirk, Garth, Joseph, Jason, and Richard. Very early in the discussion Joseph, who often assumes a summarizing where-we-are-now role, sets out the task as he sees it:

What we're really going to have to do is to come up with a little piece of railway track. Then make . . . then get a train and what you do is take pieces of wood at the bottom and put them at different spacings.

Dirk clarifies:

We could do it with a train set . . . small scale.

Joseph says, yes that was what he meant. But his formulation indicates misunder-standings the group shares – that the gaps referred to are the spaces between the wooden sleepers and that a train is needed for the experiment.

Joseph: 'You could have them 2 cms apart from each one, and you could have 5 cms apart, and see what happens.'

Dirk makes a suggestion: 'Then we could try it with different metals.' This raises in Garth's mind the question of where the metals are to come from: 'What I want to know is where we're going to get the bronze and that from. Break up our mum's antiques?'

They all laugh. This is a silly solution – but no one offers anything else. At all events his remark has the effect of focusing on the metal lines themselves, and they realize that those in their train sets are plastic.

Jason concludes: 'We'll have to make our own.' This is not very encouraging, but further complications also occur to them.

Gareth asks: 'How do we run it without electricity?' Joseph adds: 'Yes, but they'll have to have electricity wires running through them.'

But now Joseph comes in with an inspiration – a contribution from entirely outside the discussion so far: 'Hang on . . . what if it changes when things get hot or cold . . . This means we could hot up . . . then.'

Jason supports this: 'Yes use a bunsen burner to hot up the railway line to see what happens.' But Gareth is not very encouraging: 'It might melt the wheels.'

The discussion continues on these lines without getting any further. Joseph's initiative about heat is anyway finally quelled by Gareth: 'It doesn't say anything in the experiment about seeing how long it would take to melt.'

The group seek other solutions. They wish to set up a railway and alter the distances between the sleepers to see what happens when the train goes over. Joseph's initiative of things changing 'when they get hot or cold' cannot be made use of in the picture they perhaps have in their minds of their own Hornby train sets being melted by a flame from a bunsen burner. There follows reporting to the teacher of progress so far. There are some twenty exchanges during which the teacher realizes that they do not have his understanding of 'gaps'. When Dirk says: 'Why the wood's spaced out along the track, what effect they have' he choses that moment to explain: 'So the gaps are actually in the railway lines themselves. Forget the sleepers for the time being. We might be able to pick that up later.'

After this, back in their groups, the pupils can focus on the intended question. Richard has found a sentence in a book which is helpful: 'When they make railway lines, engineers must leave gaps between the rails to allow metals to expand in very hot weather.'

However, the correct formulation of the task does not help them in devising an experiment. At present they are unable to extract the essence of the problem – the expansion and contraction of metals at different temperatures – from the railway setting in which it has been placed. Gareth comes in, once again, with one of his impossible proposals: 'Or we could sneak up to the nearest railway station if we like and change the metal and see what happens.'

The others treat this with amusement, but Gareth is at least making an attempt, as before, at a problem which at present is beyond him. Joseph makes more progress by suggesting they experiment with steel, and then with other metals. Jason proclaims: 'A brainwave! That's why we must ask Mr Garfield for a list of metals he has got or can get.'

But the talk of metals is still anchored to the idea of constructing tracks. Gareth: 'It's making the tracks which is hardest.'

But they are uneasy about this. Even if it were possible to make the tracks it might not be the right way to go. As Dirk says: 'There's probably a simple way round it. We've just got to find that way.'

And Joseph adds: 'We'll probably find it in the middle of the experiment.'

But they haven't got an experiment, and they know it. Joseph, as often, sums up the situation: 'Right, so what we're really going to have to do is either Mr Garfield'll have to help us with it, or we're going to have to find another way on our own.'

Further discussion with the teacher and research worker finally enable them to symbolize the problem. Some do so earlier than others, so that when Jason formulates it for himself he gets a round of applause: 'What we've got to do really is to make two lines of metal and we'll heat them up instead of bringing a railway line. . . . We'll have to use a bunsen burner.'

Applause.

In the final discussion with the teacher prior to the experiment he deliberately reinforces its representational nature: 'If I were to give you that rod – I won't tell you what it's made of yet – let's say it's a piece of railway line.'

His intention is to lead them to the measuring of the expansion of a single rod on a gauge. But at present some of them are still thinking of a gap between two rods. John suggests: 'Cut it in half.'

But Richard and Gareth have got the point. They chorus in unison: 'There's no need to cut it in half.'

And for this group the symbolizing process is complete.

'So what would happen?' The teacher's role

For the teacher adopting a group-based approach to learning, monitoring progress may not be easy. A balance needs to be struck between allowing pupils to explore meaningful learning experiences and guiding them more directly. The question of how and when to intervene is important.

As we have seen above the teacher has an important role to play in the clarification of issues, or the supply of information. In this study the timing of interventions was facilitated by the teacher's listening to the taped discussions.

After listening to the first session he became aware of some misconceptions, and felt that a few minutes' discussion to draw together ideas would be useful, and enable him to assess whether the group were ready to try out their ideas in experimental form. In the further discussion described above he wishes to ascertain that they understand the form their experiment is going to use. He makes explicit the representational use of the rod for the line ('let's say it's a piece of railway line') and then tests further: 'What's your first task?'

And several chorus: 'To heat it up.'

The atmosphere of the teacher–group discussions is relaxed, and pupils feel free to raise questions and to explore ideas tentatively, as here where Dirk suggests that the measuring equipment (dial and pointer) could also be used to measure how far the rod 'goes back' (contracts). The pointer here moves as a cork block is pushed by the expanding metal rod.

Dirk:	Then if we leave it away . . . you'll be able to measure it . . . em . . . goes back.
Jason:	What?
Teacher:	I don't know whether that would work. Why?
Jason:	'Cause it isn't . . . there's nothing pulling it (the block).
Teacher:	Nothing pulling it. What would you have to do?
Jason:	Stick some blue tack or something on the end.
Teacher:	So what would happen?
Jason:	So that fastens to the block.

This is the first expression of interest in the contraction of metals, and the shape of a new experiment begins to emerge which the group was to pursue after this task. Similarly Jason earlier listens to the teacher's summary:

Teacher:	You've recorded an increase in the rod at the point where you heated it. Now we're talking about increase in length. Why don't you see if you can measure an increase in the length of that rod?
Dirk:	The length.
Jason:	Slowing up – 'cause you're getting heat. . . just in one place, 'cause the – really need another candle on it. The heat . . .

Joseph picks up a point, triggered by the teacher's phrase, 'recorded an increase at the point where you heated it', and grapples to express his idea that more than one localized heat source is necessary to obtain the maximum expansion.

An atmosphere where such tentative ideas can be explored is based in trust. Of paramount importance is the tact with which the teacher listens, responds, and where necessary guides the pupils' thinking through talk. A commitment to active, involved learning with regard to an individual's thinking process requires supporting, valuing and encouraging the pupils' contributions, as in the example below. Dirk and Gareth have been discussing the positioning of Jason's dial on the experimental apparatus. Gareth has reservations about the pointer method. Dirk explains to the teacher that the pointer method will work, that the pointer will act as a 'reader' which will move as the rod expands and pushes the block.

Teacher: Explain again Dirk – stick it on where?

Dirk: Well he (*Jason*) is going to stick this like so . . . and have this exactly on here.

Teacher: Pointing . . .

Dirk: There.

Teacher: Exactly so.

Dirk: So . . . will . . . how far it falls when it goes like that, like a little . . . read . . . reader . . . so it maybe goes down to there.

Teacher: Good. Yes, what do you think, Gareth?

Gareth: I think that's the case . . . but . . .

Teacher: Do you think it's going to work?

Gareth: But the block's going to be pushed along so that it'll get further and further along . . .

Dirk: Ah, I've just thought . . .

Teacher: A drawing pin might do better. That's a good point.

Gareth: It might work well that way.

Dirk: It's worth a try. We might as well try.

Here the teacher first encourages Dirk to expand, supporting him by leading words ('Pointing . . .', 'Exactly so . . .'), and asks for Gareth's opinion. Then he encourages and seeks further expansion from him ('Do you think it's going to work?) and provides positive feedback ('That's a good point'). Rather than dismissing opinions such as 'wrong' he encourages the pupils to see what happens in the experiments.

In this framework errors become part of the learning process, not to be criticized but to be learned from. In one of the early experiments the teacher noticed that the group were measuring the expansion of the width of the rod with a pair of dividers, not the length as might have been expected. He checked whether the dividers were actually measuring an increase in width. During the ensuing discussion the pupils were guided back to the question of gaps in the length, and later to the question of how to measure the length of a rod.

Interestingly the slight increase in width the group had recorded enable them to answer a question from a classmate later: 'When the rod stretches does it get thicker?' From the observation made from their 'mistake' Gareth was able to answer, 'Yes, it get's thicker. It expands all ways.'

The teacher's success in monitoring the progress of the learning was helped by an awareness of the conceptual stages the pupils had reached, obtained by the use of cassettes, and by intervening in discussions. It was also related to his sensitivity to individual thought processes through talk.

Imaginative recreation: 'What voice would I do mine in?'

Problem-solving is an activity commonly associated with mathematics or, as in the previous section, with science. But in fact it is the central activity of all serious work, though the problem may be defined very differently. In the study of literature, for instance, it is the interpretation of meaning in the text.

One way of approaching literature is through 'imaginative recreation' – that is to say a text in one medium is recreated in another (a full discussion is given in Stratta *et al.* 1973: ch. 2). Thus a short story becomes a radio or television play; an old work is restated in modern terms; a poem is enacted; a dramatic reading is given; and so on. Such an activity requires a close analysis of the meaning of the original in order to recreate it for the new medium, and this process involves interpretation and imagination.

Let us consider in more detail some work of first-year secondary school pupils aged 11–12, dramatizing for tape a small part of Ian Serraillier's *The Silver Sword*, Chapter 3, where Joseph, the Polish refugee, is hidden by an old woman when the Nazis search her cottage. (The words that become part of the play are printed in italics.)

B: I'm going to be a German.

SCRIBE: I don't want to be the old woman.

A: I'll be the old woman.

C: That'll suit you.

B: You can do the writing.

While he was away, Joseph showed the old woman the tattered photos of his family.

A: Right, we want Joseph saying these are the photos of my family or something like that – we've got to have it worked out beforehand, or else it's no good.

SCRIBE: *These are the photos of my family.*

A: This is my wife.

SCRIBE: Hang on.

A: This is my wife and these are my children.

He had taken them out of his wallet so many times to look at them that they were creased and crumpled and finger-marked all over. He spoke about his wife and children, his school, his capture by the Nazis.

B: *They're a bit tattered because I've used them.*

C: Then he would probably introduce his children and say how old they are or something like that.

SCRIBE: Yes, these are the photos of my family.

A: *When I last saw them.*

C: Just a minute, cut it there. Goodness knows where they are now.

B: They've probably grown a lot by now.

SCRIBE: *They've probably changed a lot by now.*

B: Yes because they probably

wouldn't have proper food.

A: What've you got?

SCRIBE: *These are the photos of my family when I last saw them. They've probably changed a lot by now.*

A: This is my wife.

B: No, it's got to be the old woman now.

C: She's pretty, she's pretty.

A: I'd like that dress.

B: She's trying to comfort him now see.
(Agreement)

A: Then the man, Joseph, introduces his family. This is Jan . . .
(Disagreement)
This is Edek, this is Bronia, this is Ruth.

C: They're all very nice – the old woman.

B: No, she'd say, I'm sure they're all very nice.

A: She could say, *what lovely children.*

B: What voice would I do mine in?

A: Joseph?

B: Yes.

A: Getting slow – you've got to make it clear.

C: Sound sorry, you know, you haven't seen her for years.

The transcription reproduces the main lines of the dialogue. It is at once clear that the pupils are engaged in an exercise which is both interpretative and creative. Not only do they have to answer for themselves questions about character (of the order of 'What does this person feel?') and about the text (of the order of why the word 'changed' and not 'grown' applies to the children), but also they actually have to pose these questions themselves. And they have to do so because they are required to use the words, enact the character. One boy asks, 'What voice would I do mine in?' This requires them to think further of the nature of the emotion involved, and the reasons for it – 'Sound sorry, you know, you haven't seen her for years.' They are recognizing the emotion behind the words: there are two suggestions for what the old woman says on seeing the wife's picture: 'she's pretty', 'I'd like that dress', and they are all happy to agree when one pupil verbalizes their reason for such words: 'She's trying to comfort him now see.'

So far they have only been concerned with a few lines of the story, but profitably concerned, because the interpretation of narrative into speech is the central process in the exercise. And, as we have seen, they are conscious that they are not producing *written* dialogue – it has to be spoken. We see this again in the discussion prompted by the opening sentence of the next paragraph.

| The old woman was moved by his story. | C: Think of something for the old woman; she was moved by his story.
A: I feel very sorry for you.
C: But you've got to get the right sort of voice for that.
A: I feel very sorry, I wish I could do something for you.
B: I know, she could have said: It must have been horrible. Have a bit of food – would you like some food to cheer you up? |

The group is seeking out language for the old woman's sympathy. They are not satisfied with the first suggestion, but perhaps if it is said with appropriate feeling that will help. Even so the words aren't strong enough – but if she expresses a desire to help that will be better. ('I feel very sorry, I wish I could do something for you.') The last speaker both strengthens the expression of sympathy, and gives embodiment to the help ('It must have been horrible. Have a bit of food – would you like some food to cheer you up?') By doing this the pupils have realized the significance of a line of narrative which might not have been dwelt on in silent reading.

The activity of re-creation in radio form was new to the pupils but it is clear that they were learning rapidly, both about the nature of the original novel, and the nature of the radio medium. The next step was to make a rough taped version for this revealed defects (and virtues) which could not have been predicted by the pupils themselves at the earlier stage. In the story there is a knock on the door and the old woman hides Joseph up the chimney before admitting the two Nazi soldiers to search the house.

| 'Quick – up there!' The old woman pointed up the chimney. 'There's an opening on the right, half-way up.'

Joseph dived into the hearth and hauled himself up over the iron spit. The fire was only smouldering and there was not much smoke. He had not found the opening when the door | OLD WOMAN: Quick, up the chimney. There's an opening half-way up on the right. Quickly. I'm coming.
GERMAN: Out of my way Polish dog.
OLD WOMAN: What do you want?
GERMAN: You heard the prison bell didn't you? We're searching for an escaped prisoner. |

burst open and two soldiers came in.
While they searched the room, he stood
very still, his legs astride the chimney.
He wanted to cough. He thought his
lungs would burst.

OLD WOMAN: Please don't make a mess.

The characters are well imagined; notice for instance the 'natural' reaction of the proud housewife to the business of the soldier: 'Please don't make a mess.' The soldiers wishing to search the chimney proved less successful:

'What about the chimney?' said a
German voice.
'Plenty of room to hide up there.'
'Plenty of soot too,' said the other
soldier. 'Your uniform's older than
mine. What about you going up?'
'Not likely.'
'Then we'll send a couple of bullets
up for luck.'
Two ear-splitting explosions. It
seemed as if the whole chalet was falling down. Joseph clung on to his perch.
There was a great tumbling about his
ears. He clung and clung and clung –
till his fingers were torn from their grip,
and he fell.
When he came to his senses, he was
lying on the floor. The old woman was
bending over him, washing his face with
cold water.
'It's all right – they've gone,' she said.
'The fall of soot saved you. The soldiers
ran for it when the soot came down.
They were afraid for their uniforms.'

GERMAN: What about the chimney?
2 GERMAN: You search, your uniform is
older than mine.
GERMAN: Not likely.
2 GERMAN: We'll send a couple of
bullets up for luck.
JOSEPH: Oh my ears!
(Pause)
OLD WOMAN: It's all right now, they've
gone. The fall of soot saved you.

It is clear that here the dialogue is not communicating the amount of information necessary, and in any case it is far too bare – the incident is over before it generates any tension. On the tape Joseph and the old woman seem to be talking in the presence of the soldiers; there are technical matters to be learnt which would help, but the fundamental problem is that the pupils are conceiving largely in visual terms and not in terms of sound alone. They are not realizing how little of what is in the book and in their visual imagination their words are conveying. One obvious step in such work is for each group to consider its own tape in detail with a view to improving on it. As with all such work, whether the teacher decides to let them do this or to give them another piece of the novel to which to apply the lessons learnt is, of course, a matter for individual judgement.

To intervene?

Small-group work is important in all subjects. Active learning, the developing of research techniques, problem-solving, co-operating, more space for individual contributions – these things are manifest in the two lessons we have looked at. But teachers are not therefore redundant. They create the situation, set the problem, monitor the progress, decide when and what sort of intervention is necessary. (See e.g. Wade 1985: 13–20.) Mr Garfield, the science teacher, listens to the group on tape so that he can assess the learning, and consider when he must reformulate the problem for them, and prompt them towards abstracting it from the literal 'railway trains' setting.

Mr Reid, the English teacher, lets the work on the radio play go on a long time. And in fact he will let them attempt to perform the script they have produced. It is then, with their realization of its limitations before them, that he will begin to ask questions which guide their thinking towards new solutions.

Mr Garfield could have told his groups about the expansion of metals. Mr Reid could have played his groups a professional radio play and started from there. On other occasions they might have done so: on this one they did not. Their reasons for that must lie in their view of the value of the process as well as of the product.

8 · Adolescents arguing

DEBORAH BERRILL

Adolescence brings with it new cognitive capabilities and a new shaping of the individual identity. Parents and teachers alike feel the results of weightier and more outspoken argument as adolescents strike out against authority, especially in personal attempts to make their own sense of their developing lives. However, these same characteristics, often viewed in a negative sense by adults, offer special opportunities for affective and cognitive development.

When we speak of adolescents' capabilities for argument we often conjure scenes of oral exchange in which individuals bludgeon each other with verbal clubs, blocking the ideas of opponents before they are received and rather blindly striking out with blows of their own. This type of argument rarely develops either cognitive or affective dimensions of anyone involved – at any age. Rather individuals usually become more entrenched in their own positions and feel increasingly isolated from those with opposing views. This is certainly not what we wish to foster.

What do we mean by oral argument?

Argument as a type of discussion

Instead of condoning assertive pummelling, we wish to develop the kind of argument that Dixon and Stratta (1986) propose when they suggest an open form of argument which includes discussion. They refer to 'a group of people working collaboratively to think through a choice of action or belief' and further clarify this notion by saying:

> The kinds of process we are thinking of include raising questions heuristically, examining and critically scrutinising alternative positions, making tentative pro- posals, investigating and studying the grounds for generalised opinions, coming to conclusions or deciding that the issue cannot be completely resolved for the moment.
>
> (Dixon and Stratta 1986: 10)

In oral argument, then, we are looking for a critical examination of ideas. If we understand argument as a specific type of discussion which has logical exploration of ideas as its essence (Wilkinson 1986a), we set certain expectations for the processes involved. As Britton (1986) says, rather than flat contradiction and abuse, we are looking for mutually supportive environments in which ideas can be explored.

Argument as a search for truth

With argument we are concerned with the notion of truthfulness. Bruner (1986) explores this idea when he differentiates between narrative and argument:

> A good story and a well-formed argument are different natural kinds. Both can be used as a means for convincing another. Yet what they convince *of* is fundamentally different: arguments convince one of their truth, stories of their lifelikeness.
>
> (Bruner 1986: 11)

Popper and Eccles (1981) also look to a use of language which differentiates between truth and falsehood. They conjure a scene of early humans who huddle in their cave, crowding about the fire, telling stories of their recent hunting expeditions and the animals that 'got away'. Referring to this use of language as descriptive, they write

> However, the interesting thing is that the descriptive function of language brings with it the basis for the argumentative function of language, and for a critical attitude towards language. Just the very fact that lying becomes possible means that for obvious practical and adaptational reasons it is important . . . to distinguish between truth and falsehood. It is just for this very reason that we have built into us the need to develop criticism and the need to develop a critical attitude towards a report, and with it, the need to develop an argumentative language – a language in which the truth of a report can be criticized or attacked, or in which it can be defended by supplementary reports. That . . . marks the beginning of argument in human language.
>
> (Popper and Eccles 1981: 456)

Argument involves a critical analysis of ideas which attempts to delineate the truthfulness of those ideas. This logical activity manifests itself at its most formal in written argument, which incorporates a thesis in the Aristotelian sense and a series of ideas which support the thesis and are shown to be related both to the thesis and to each other.

However, we don't expect this kind of structure in oral argument. Oral argument attempts to get at the truth, but in a much more exploratory fashion incorporating a wider range of thinking activities, including the use of common sense and intuition, or in Bruner's words, 'the ability to see possible formal connections before one is able to prove them in any formal way' (Bruner 1986: 13).

In oral argument we do find an appeal to common sense and a use of intuitive response which we do not expect to find in written argument. Our hope with oral argument is that participants will evaluate the truthfulness of various types of evidence, of generalizations and of hypotheses being offered.

Argument emphasizes difference

In argument, then, we are seeking to understand different points of view and to evaluate those different approaches to the issue at hand. Even everyday use of the word 'argument' carries this 'difference of opinion' essence of the word. However, much everyday argument accentuates just that there are differences rather than stressing that resolution of the differences is best achieved through first *understanding* the differences. In oral argument, we hope that the resolution of difference occurs through appreciating the differences, through recognizing the validities of other approaches.

Valuing and eliciting differences

Before different points of view can be evaluated, they must receive recognition and be valued for the validities they hold. This means that participants must feel comfortable enough with a group to offer their own ideas and to seek ideas from others in the group.

How idealistic is this premise? Let us look at the argument of 16-year-olds engaged in discussing the question, 'Should parents be able to control the lives of their teenaged children?' The following extract is from the very opening of the conversation.

> *Leanne:* Do your parents rule your life, Bimal?
> *Bimal:* Most of the time, yeh.
> *Leanne:* So what kind of things do they tell you to do then?
> *Bimal:* Er, lay the table.
> *Leanne:* Is that it? Oh, goodness.
> *Bimal:* Near enough. They tell me off for small reasons like talking back to my dad.
> *Leanne:* My mum started shouting at me 'cos I was an hour late. (*Laughter*) It isn't as though I . . .
> *Stephen:* That's right . . . look, you've (*??*)
> *Leanne:* I know. Oh, who cares? (*More laughter*) You know the other night . . . on Wednesday. . . . Right, you know that Wednesday, Bimal?
> *Bimal:* Yeh.
> *Leanne:* Right. I was supposed to go home at nine, right.
> *Stephen:* How embarrassing then.
> *Leanne:* I arrived home at ten o'clock and my mum started moaning at me . . . she's gonna ban me from going out.
> *Bimal:* I come home at ten and she didn't say a word to me.
> *Leanne:* Didn't she?
> *Bimal:* (*Mumble*)
> *Leanne:* Sheryl, what are your parents like with you?

Sheryl: (*Mumble*)
Stephen: Do they rule you?
Sheryl: No.
Stephen: Not even most of the time?
Sheryl: No.
Leanne: You've got it easy then.

Even at this early stage in the discussion, the participants are eager to hear different points of view. Leanne actively seeks different responses of various group members, asking them by name for their contributions. The question they are discussing may be one in which different points of view or different practices have extra appeal due to the potential personal usefulness of the information. Regardless, however, it is worth noting that these adolescents deliberately seek alternate views from group members and that they receive those views, recognizing their validity and the validity of each individual's own experience.

Although this conversation focuses on personal experience over the two days that the pupils had for discussion time, the participants periodically attempt to generalize as we see in the continuation of the above extract.

(Several minutes later in the discussion)
Bimal: Right, go on then. Should they be able to control our lives?
Stephen: Er, yes and no. Yes they should and no they shouldn't 'cos it's our life in'it? When we get married we're not gonna have all the time to do what we want, are we? So let's (?) now while we can.
Sheryl: I think if you tell them what time you're coming in it doesn't matter so much.
Leanne: It does.
Sheryl: Well not so much. At least you're with someone. If you're by yourself you should come in earlier.
Leanne: My mum waits up for me, she does. This is my mum . . . she waits up for me. Like she says, 'If you're going out tonight', she says, 'I'm not gonna wait up for you.' 'All right then, I don't mind.' She waits up for me. Sick!
Bimal: Next question (??)
Stephen: We've just heard that.
Sheryl: What was the question?
Stephen: Go on.
Bimal: You said they should and they shouldn't, right. So when should they tell you?
Stephen: Not all the time but most of the time. Now and again.
Bimal: Yeh, when?
Stephen: All right. If you're going out to a disco or something, somewhere like that . . . if you're just going out with your mates, then it's different in'it . . . what time . . .
Leanne: Yeh, but do you have arguments with your parents?
Stephen: Yeh, with my dad I do.

Bimal's attempts to elicit generalizations are not particularly successful here and the conversation tends to return to concrete specifics with Leanne's 'Yeh, but do you have arguments with your parents?'. Certainly once adolescents elicit and receive ideas different from their own, they need to be encouraged to develop generalizations and to evaluate the validity of the generalizations. This particular argumentative conversation would be, stronger if there were a more complete evaluation of the different approaches given, along with an attempt to come to generalizations based on the personal experiences related. The great strength on which these particular individuals could build, however, is their recognition and valuing of their differences.

Challenging ideas without criticizing people

Another group of 16-year-olds had a quite different conversation about the same topic. Samantha, Divina, Pallvi and Belinda have been talking for about ten minutes at the time the following extract occurs.

Divina: What things should the parents not allow their children to do?

Pallvi: Like they should see who they're going out with, you know. Not going out but I mean like who they're hanging around with.

Belinda: Yeh, but it's like . . . say . . . right, that you've got a boyfriend and your mum didn't like him . . . are you gonna stop?

Pallvi: No.

Belinda: Exactly. So why are you saying that you want your parents to see what you're doing?

Pallvi: No, I mean . . . like . . . not about your boyfriends . . . the people you hang around with. . . . Boyfriend or your friends.

Here, generalizations are made and individual response is used for verifying the generalization. Belinda hypothesizes a situation to challenge Pallvi's generalization that parents 'should see who [teenagers are] going out with'. Belinda's challenge is of the idea, not of Pallvi, and Pallvi accepts the validity of Belinda's challenge and attempts to clarify her generalization. This group accepts their different points of view and goes on to generalize and to evaluate the generalizations made.

This group is composed of four pupils from three different cultural and racial backgrounds – Asian, Afro-Caribbean and Anglo-Saxon – and the participants explicitly refer to their differences in exploring issues of parental control. The above conversation continues, still focusing on the situation of parental role in sanctioning friendships. After some intervening talk, the discussion is as follows:

Pallvi: No, like, you look at your friends in one way, don't you, say like you know 'em 'cos you talk to them all the time but your parents hardly know that person, do they?

Divina: They just look on the outward view of the person.

Pallvi: Yeh. So they can't really exactly say, 'You can't hang around with them', can they?

Belinda: They can if they . . .

Divina: Well if they've got . . . I know . . . but it depends on the person . . . let's

	say if your parents have got a lot of influence on you then you'd listen to them if they say that.
Pallvi:	Sometimes it's blackmail.
Samantha:	If my mum said, 'I don't like your friend' then that's it . . . she don't like my friend.
Divina:	No, but if you know really that your friend is good and she's not a bad person. . . .
Pallvi:	Yeh, but you'd have to try and prove it to your parents wouldn't you, that they weren't bad?
Samantha:	No . . . they'd prove it then wouldn't they?
Divina:	I know, right, that if I wanted to do something and my parents did not agree I wouldn't feel right going out and doing it.
Pallvi:	Yeh, but I mean you've gotta . . . like . . . see what it's like . . . to go out and see what it's like but your parents are going to keep you in all the time.
Belinda:	Yeh.
Divina:	So you mean that children should have a chance to go and do whatever their parents say they shouldn't do?

During this part of the conversation, the pupils generalize and speculate, attempting to convince each other by extending the speculations through to their consequences, consequences which seem to be firmly rooted in their own experience. It is Divina, especially, who does this when she says, 'if your parents have got a lot of influence on you then you'd listen to them' and 'if I wanted to do something and my parents did not agree I wouldn't feel right going out and doing it'. In attempting to convince Pallvi of the fallacy of her generalization, Divina explicitly pushes the generalization to its logical conclusion when she says, 'So you mean that children should have a chance to go and do whatever their parents say they shouldn't do?'

The cultural differences which are only implicit in this part of the conversation and which underlie the different responses of the pupils are made explicit about ten minutes later.

Pallvi:	It's like . . . you know . . . this dinner pass thing, right? My dad didn't agree with it . . .
Samantha:	I mean my mum signed it (?).
Pallvi:	But when he says, 'Oh no, you can't 'cos there's boys round these days' . . . I mean if you're gonna learn to go out, I mean, you might as well . . . you know, what harm can you . . .
Belinda:	I mean like if you go out in a group and that . . . but they don't really, like my parents, they don't understand that.
Pallvi:	'Cos like I'm a different thing . . . like I'm not an English person, right, so I mean you could think of a different (?). Different nationalities they think of it in different ways. Get what I mean?
Divina:	I think so.
Pallvi:	Like Indian people . . . they are so cautious, you know what I mean. You know . . . like you know . . . I mean I'm Indian . . . so like my parents . . .

Divina: Would your parents stop you from going out with a boy?

Pallvi: As long as they knew who it was.

Divina: So you're allowed to have boyfriends.

Pallvi: Yes, but I mean if I went out with an English guy they would feel bad about it but they know that it's me that's gonna get into trouble.

Samantha: Well why do they feel bad about you going out with English guys?

Pallvi: No, they don't mind me going round with ... but if they like saw me going out with an English boy ... now wouldn't you feel bad about it if you went out with an Indian boy and your parents ... I mean I don't feel bad about it but your parents would feel bad themselves.

Belinda: My sister has got several boyfriends who are coloured and several who are white and several who are Chinese.

Pallvi: Yeh I know, but I mean like when you think of it in a different way thinking it's all right ... I mean ... you know ... we're not doing anything bad, we're not gonna (?). But they think of it in a way that ... oh what if like my gran saw me going out with an English bloke, what would she think?

(Several minutes pass with continued discussion on dating people of other races)

Divina: Well maybe they think that if you mix more with let's say an English person you'll lose your culture.

Pallvi: I know I'm not gonna lose it so ...

Divina: Yeh but they're probably not so sure about it though 'cos if you marry out you're sure to lose bits of it.

Pallvi: No, with us, see, we've got so many people that have married out in different castes you don't mind it.

The mutual support and openness in exploration of controversial topics here is quite extraordinary. It is obvious that the students are learning new information about each other and that they are each willing to share their differences. The climate is a supportive one which is shown through the fact that the participants offer information which potentially leaves them vulnerable, just because their ways are different. It is curiosity about and acceptance of their differences that enables the talk to develop in the manner it does.

A distinctive feature of this oral argument is the way in which these adolescents probe and challenge each others' ideas in a climate of collaboration. Participants challenge ideas without criticizing the person who presented those ideas. Divina's speculations are not meant to be personal, nor are they taken by Pallvi to be personal. Instead, there is a mutual exploration of the truths associated with maintenance of a minority culture in a different cultural mainstream.

The extending of information and the probing of validities is received by all. Looking just at initial words of contributions, one is aware of the constant evaluation of statements that is going on. We see phrases such as, 'Yeh, but you'd ...', 'No, they'd prove ...', 'So you mean ...', 'Well why ...', 'No they don't ...', and 'Well maybe they think ...'. These openings of responses show the challenging of ideas which is occurring in this conversation. This is certainly argumentative talk of the nature we hope to see: an exploration of differences first through receiving and acknowledging the validities of the differences and then through evaluating the information received.

Qualities of information

We expect that people of different ages will argue the same question in quite different ways. Part of this may surely be due to life experience; those who have lived longer bring in a greater quantity of experience for evidence. However, another difference in the quality of argument depends on the *quality* of evidence offered. Students in their final year of university in Ontario, Canada, were asked to discuss the same question, 'Should parents be able to control the lives of their teenaged children?' The conversations that emerged with the 22-year-olds reflect a level of abstraction which we do not expect of 16-year-olds but which give an indication of the kind of development we might encourage with our adolescents.

The conversation of Catherine, Stephen and Gary opens in the following way:

Catherine: So where does one begin?
  (*Pause*)
Catherine: Should we read the question first? That's always a good idea. (*Reading*) 'Should parents be able to control the lives of their teenaged children?'
Stephen: Hmm.
Catherine: It seems to me that control is a . . . a big word. I mean like what kind of percentage are we talking here? . . . In terms of . . .
Gary: And teenage is a big word too.
Catherine: Yeh.
Gary: Thirteen and nineteen are quite different.
Stephen: Lives is also a big word.
Catherine:
Stephen: }(*Laughter*)
Gary:
Stephen: Let's see, okay.
Gary: My pen . . .
Stephen: Hmm. Well, I think . . . uhm . . . I, I immediately think . . . that there's, there's . . . in terms of, of parents controlling lives of teenage children I think there are at least uhm two . . . two areas of responsibility . . . that, that parents will enforce on children . . . or . . . hmm . . .
  (*Pause*)
  Yes. Uhm. I think of the simple rules like uhm making sure that children get homework done . . . uhm going to bed, who children can see and can't see are the . . . is the first paradigm of responsibility but the second one is one which the children will have to formulate within that area of responsibility, within that area of . . . control. So that children who live in disagreement with their parents will be able to . . . uhm formulate their own code of responsibility. So I . . . I mean I'm thinking of me as a child having to live in silence about so many things . . . uhm . . . and . . . and in order to please my parents on one level and in order to exemplify the

responsibilities they were placing on me . . . uhm . . . I could . . . I could . . . uhm, I could easily live by those rules. But what was always more important for me was the kind of responsibilities that . . . or the kinds of rules that I would place on myself that would always be . . . outside of my parents. So do you see what I'm saying? That there are two kinds of responsibilities, there are two . . . there are two ways of dealing with the control that parents expect of us.

Even in these opening minutes of conversation, we can see that a climate of mutual support and valuing of each other's contributions exists, for Stephen's long contribution occurs without interruption. The others are receptive to what he has to say and are willing to listen through his hesitations until he is able to formulate his response.

However, we also see in these opening minutes a different qualitative level of information being discussed. The 16-year-olds discussed the question either from a very concrete level ('your parents', 'my mum', 'Do they rule you') or from an abstract level which was a generalization of their experience. And this is completely appropriate. We see that we can encourage their cognitive development by stretching them from their own personal experiences to a consideration of abstract syntheses of those experiences. The young adults also work from personal experience, but their generalizations and speculations transcend the particular in a very different way. Stephen hypothesizes two types of control: he categorizes his abstractions into a higher level abstraction, an exploration of the idea of control. This, in turn, was the implied direction of Catherine's opening contribution, 'It seems to me that control is a . . . a big word.'

In fact, the two hours of conversation of this group focuses in large part on the definition of 'control' and on the moral implications of any person controlling any other person. As well, the participants probe each other's underlying assumptions in an attempt to come to agreement about what they are discussing. At one stage, they discuss the idea of authority and whether or not that might be closer to an idea of control which is acceptable to them.

Stephen: No, I thought because I'm not necessarily thinking of authority in negative terms, I'm thinking of influence . . . I'm thinking of example . . . and I'm thinking of . . .

Catherine: A guiding factor almost?

Stephen: Because as a child . . .

Gary: What was that?

Catherine: A guiding factor.

(*Stephen gives an anecdote about growing up and looking to his parents for authority*)

Gary: This . . . this is just a slight offshoot of that. In my . . . in my vast experience I find generally fathers don't really relate very well . . . not don't relate very well but play a secondary role . . . to their, uh, teenaged children. I wonder why that is, too.

Stephen: But you see I think that's part of it. I think, and I don't mean to be giving the definitive answer, but I think that's part of the problem. That's what I mean when I was questioning families, too, because I think a part of the way the family's set up is that the man will go . . . the man has very definite responsibilities with the children which usually circle around absence. The father is mostly not there. But that's the very extreme example of the nuclear family, I think. In many ways fathers are becoming closer with their children now, I think.

Catherine: Right. I just find it kind of ironic, because I can see where you're coming from about being a secondary type force and in my own background it's very much my mother that I would turn to if there were any situations. But it comes back to me now that it was always my father who was the one who was the guiding factor, be it through my mother or directly. . . . I have examples of where I was having problems with school work and I was feeling very pressured by it. Somehow I wasn't even realizing that I was making it known, but at the supper table I would say now the teacher really bothered me today with demands and my father would be the one who secretly, without me knowing, called that teacher and said 'You know I'm really concerned, you know . . . this is obviously affecting my daughter and I'm concerned.' Which blew me away when I found out three weeks later that my father had done this because I thought what happened in my life was almost irrelevant to what was happening . . . to him. But it did have a factor and he . . . he was . . .

Stephen: He was very private about the way he dealt with this.

Catherine: Yes, exactly, whereas my mother was much more vocal or was more sympathetic, the one who would have the hugs, whereas my father would be more distant but he was the one who would make more the major changes I guess that came about in my life.

Stephen: But it's still interesting the way he would relate too to you in that fashion when you didn't know that he was having that kind of influence over you.

Catherine: So there's an example, I guess, of some type of control and yet it's certainly not a damaging one. If anything it was to help me.

Gary: So it's obvious that there are many ways of controlling people.

Catherine: Yes.

In this extract, the speakers use personal experience to challenge generalizations of others. Catherine is cognizant before she relates her anecdote that it refutes generalizations just made by both Gary and Stephen. However, she doesn't say that their generalizations are without validity; rather, she introduces her evidence as 'ironic', stressing the difference of opinions. As well, many of the contributions are tentative, including 'I think' or including a re-phrasing of strongly stated positions such as Gary's 'I find generally fathers don't really relate very well . . . not don't relate very well but play a secondary role . . .'. The explicit tentativeness or ongoing modification of positions keeps exploration of a topic open even when there is acknowledged difference of opinion.

Besides incorporating a different quality of information, this argument of young adults also incorporates a different quality of evaluation. The ongoing evaluation of contributions which we saw emerging in the discussion of Divina, Pallvi, Samantha and Belinda is extended here. In both cases the participants challenge ideas without criticizing the people who presented the ideas. The difference in this last group is that the ideas are of such a different quality in their more complex abstractions that the evaluation is also of a cognitively more complex nature. For instance, Stephen, Catherine and Gary have a brief exploration of the issue of parental control of friends, but their conversation is quite different from that of the 16-year-olds.

Stephen: I'm thinking that maybe there are good things with what we see as negative authority because later in life when we do go back and question that kind of authority we recognize that our sense of social responsibility comes out of, you know, comes out of that structure where we begin to feel responsible for so many things that we couldn't be responsible for when we were younger, that our parents wouldn't. . . . What, what would you do if uh . . . what do you think is the kind of authority in which the father and mother will say you can't see so and so, I don't want you involved with him or her until you are about 16.

Catherine: I have difficulty with that. And I guess it stems from why the parents don't want them to see that individual. If it's for racist reasons, then I'd have a great deal of difficulty with that.

Stephen: So you see that's why you would become more socially responsible later on, too. I mean, that's what I mean by the good things coming out of it as well. Do you see? I mean . . .

The issue of parental control of friends is used by the older speakers as an example of larger issues underlying parental control whereas it is seen as one of the primary issues by the 16-year-olds. A different sort of truth is being sought by the older group than by the younger group. This is especially apparent later in the conversation of the older group. After Catherine's contribution above, the conversation includes a number of topics which revolve around the issue of authority, including sharing a house with parents and the need for 'support' and 'guidance' rather than for 'authority'. Fifteen minutes after the last extract, the conversation returns to Catherine's anecdote.

Gary: And also actually, with your father phoning the teacher. . . . I mean it's a very roundabout way of doing it and a very good way of doing it too.

Catherine: And now I can look back. At the time I was very hurt by that. It was like how could you have done that? You know, it was bothering me but I can deal with it on my own. But I realized later when the teacher approached me about it that I wasn't dealing with it on my own, and my father could see that and the concern came through. But that's where the communication is funny, because I guess my father and I were communicating in this particular situation, except that I wasn't viewing it in that sense. He was able to tell just from some of my terse remarks that were coming out that I was not happy, but I guess I just didn't sit down and say, 'Dad I've got a problem here'. You know, like (?).

Gary: Perhaps he also sensed because of your terseness that if he did say, Cathy, I'll go talk to the man, you'd say no, no, no, it's my life. I don't know. Quite frankly I'm terrified of being a parent and this isn't helping me. So none of us like the word control . . . so we'll get rid of that.

[. . .]

Stephen: . . . I'm thinking too of the *Sammy and Rosie* film and at the end, well throughout the film in fact, the issue of control is an important one and there are families represented . . . and the interesting thing about Sammy and Rosie too is that families take on larger social significances so that Raffie the father in the film is also the leader of the country. And at the end of the film Margaret Thatcher is speaking. Margaret Thatcher's voice comes over on to the screen and the black people are being kicked out of their camp and new parliament buildings are being constructed. And we hear Margaret Thatcher saying, 'We all want unity. We all want peace.' And what she's saying is . . . she's including . . . she's telling the audience and the nation that everybody wants the same thing and in fact what we are seeing is that in fact that's not true and . . . but . . . because she's in this authoritative position she can erase such differences and say that unity . . . she can believe, and I think she in fact does, that what she wants is best for everybody and that everybody should want these things. And I think it's true. I think that parents know what they want from us and that their definitions from very early on are going to be things that we will have to react against later on. But those processes are important. In the film too it's important too that we hear Margaret Thatcher say that . . . and we see the people being . . . uhm . . . thrown out of the camp, but we also know that they're going to reconstruct the camp, and that they're going to, you know, they're going to keep being politically involved against that. But the fact is that they're working, they're still working within that structure . . . they have to. It . . . it seems to me . . . it seems to me that . . . umm . . . one of the really interesting things, and . . . and, again it might seem not to have anything to do with it but it does umm . . .

Gary: He's been talking a long time.

Catherine: (*Laughter*)

Stephen: Sorry, I'll stop in a minute, but, uhmm . . . uhm . . . uh . . . politics like feminism couldn't exist without . . . umm . . . without . . . without a patriarchy. Umm . . . and there are . . . there are glories and we . . . I mean there are glories within feminism but interestingly enough it exists only because of the patriarchy. So what I am saying is that I think . . . I think that . . . that the control our parents exert over us can include . . . um . . . many of the beautiful things that we become in reaction against that too. (*Pause*) Do you think?

Gary: I think feminism would fall into the category of . . . umm . . . to quote my friend Karl Marx, dialectical materialism . . . umm . . . you know, every . . . ah . . . action breeds a reaction.

For the 22-year-olds, conversation that began as anecdote and as generalized discussion about types of parental control has broadened into issues regarding the morality of anyone controlling anyone else and into speculations regarding dialectical materialism and 'negative' authoritative actions which may cause positive reactions in response. These speakers are very conscious of the fact that they are meant to be discussing 'parental control' and they explicitly relate their comments back to that topic, trying to ensure that other participants understand how the broadened conversation incorporates the initial task.

Without a doubt, there is a different quality of information and speculation in this conversation than there was in that of the 16-year-olds. The 16-year-olds discuss the question in abstract terms of parents and teenagers in general, whereas the young adults discuss the original question in the more abstract context of any individual exerting control over any other individual. Although the 16-year-olds do speculate about points of view of persons other than themselves (Pallvi's 'gran' for instance), they rely primarily on their own experience for evidence. The 22-year-olds, on the other hand, bring in external evidence of art (the film, *Sammy and Rosie*) and philosophical treatise.

By helping pupils to become aware of their own talk regarding the quality of information they use and the quality of validity claims they make, we can facilitate their continual growth. Integral to development in this regard is the increasing ability to evaluate both the quality of information and the validity of ideas being discussed. This is the goal of argument: to bring a variety of approaches to an initial question or problem and to evaluate the truthfulness of each in order to come up with a 'best' solution, either individually or as a group.

Acknowledgements

I wish to thank Mrs Bettina Kulsdom at Norbury Manor High School for Girls, Thornton Heath, Surrey, and Mrs Maureen Lippett at Lanfranc High School, Croydon, Surrey, who welcomed me into their classrooms and shared my enthusiasm for learning from the pupils. The work is impossible of course without the pupils themselves at Norbury Manor, Lanfranc High School, and Trent University in Peterborough, Canada, all of whom participated in the research and the task with seriousness and industry.

I wish also to thank the Social Sciences and Humanities Research Council of Canada and Trent University, Canada, for research grants which supported this work.

9 Rules and roles in discussion

ANDREW WILKINSON with GILL SHEA
and GEOFFREY ROBINSON

Introduction

In story-telling there are basically one rule and one role. The rule is that the story-teller speaks and the others listen; the role is that the speaker is 'dominant'. There is the same situation in other 'long turns' – giving an extended account, explanation, and so on. On the other hand in conversation and discussion, marked by reciprocal 'short turns', there are a variety of rules and a variety of roles. The basic *rule* is to take turns, but there are many others. There is not one basic *role*: a participant may move through several – from leading to passive – in the space of a few minutes.

Rules in discussion

In conversation at the level of 'chat' or 'gossip' there is usually no intention of discussing any particular topic with a view to reaching a conclusion. The participants want to feel that they have made a contribution and they are unhappy if someone dominates or constantly interrupts. They need to know how much to say, when to be silent, when to drop a topic if the others are glassy-eyed or their attention is distracted. They are usually tolerant when someone is not clear, and wait while they rephrase. Or if someone breaks down they may attempt help by formulating the sentence they think is intended.

The employment of discussion techniques in schools is not normally agenda-free in this kind of way, and quite properly so. One of the main functions of 'conversation' as we have outlined it above is to preserve consensus, to confirm people in their security, to further social coherence, and to that end many clichés are exchanged about the weather, cats, children, slimming and health foods. Above all it is not meant to challenge. In schools the avowed intention is to stimulate and challenge, so commonly discussions are exploratory or task-oriented.

In such discussions the rules, usually more assumed than taught, are of the following kind. Take turns; don't interrupt; don't overtalk; share out the talk time; don't allow silence; don't speak at too great a length; listen to others; respect their point of view; find rational reasons for agreeing or dissenting; respond to the merits, not demerits, of others' points; do not be personal; be objective; be positive and constructive; be co-operative; try to arrive at a mutually satisfying conclusion. The consensus may be challenged, but with the intention of arriving at a new consensus by rational argument.

The very listing of these rules however brings out how limited they are. For one thing they are culturally determined. In Antigua it is common for several people to speak at once throughout a whole conversation; with Lapps, Danes, and the Western Apache it is quite normal for the participants to fall silent (Crystal 1987: 177). For another they have less reality in the world of business and politics. This is because the opposing principle to consensus, or 'solidarity' as it is often called in this context, is not rational challenge but 'power'. In educational discussions in schools, colleges and universities the rules listed above are normally observed and advocated. They are rules of 'solidarity', not in that they enable clichés to be exchanged (far from it) but in the sense that they confirm individuals in their feeling of the value of their contributions. They are supported by age-old beliefs that individuals of good will may by the processes of reason discover the truth.

Discussions based on 'power', however, have an agenda which assumes that the truth has already been discovered and it is the role of the meeting to support it or facilitate its implementation. Thus the chair of a business or political meeting will be skilled in cutting short or not 'hearing' dissenting comments, in summarizing from a discussion only favourable points, in ruling inconvenient matters 'out of order'. Such persons might be using the usual rules to their advantage. However in some cases they might reverse them: DO NOT listen; DO NOT respect others' points of view; DO be personal; DO arrive at a consensus – by force not by consent. Interestingly one of the reasons that breaking these rules work so well is that most people have expectations that discussion will be fair, that people will be courteous, that individual viewpoints will be respected. They thus have no counter when confronted by aggression and rudeness, naked or covert. It would be absurd to pretend that all educational discussions are of the former kind, and all others of the latter. But because of the relative weighings of 'solidarity' and 'power' in each situation that must be the trend.

The conclusion to be drawn from this analysis is not that teachers should advocate the breaking of the rules. ('How often have I told you to interrupt?') Because the rules are ultimately based on respect for other people, and for the validity of reason – the two bases of civilization – teachers have no choice but to teach them. But what we must teach our students also is awareness of these breaches – so that they are not taken by surprise, so that they may learn the counters, so that they discern the nature of the strategies of the public figure interviewed on television, and remember the ballot box.

Roles in discussion

In social life roles are of various kinds. They may have a biological origin – sex, age, family position or race. They may have a hierarchical basis, such as rank in the army, seniority in business, class in society at large. They may have a meritocratic basis, where the more able people attain the higher position. They may have a personal basis – people with a certain type of personality may claim status or leadership, or alternatively shun it. Any individual role has several bases – one person may be male, unable, self-effacing, lower class: another may be female, high-ranking, able, and of a forceful personality.

It is thus impossible to have a role which does not in some sense stem from biological and social sources. What is important, however, is that those roles should not become stereotypes and therefore disabling. Thus the aspirations of girls may be limited very early by the role-models they are presented with in their reading, as well as by child-rearing practices. Thus the abilities of older people, which could be developed to the great benefit of all, often go to seed when society hints in all kinds of subtle ways that they are 'past it' or 'over the hill'. The development of children may be damaged when they are compared unfavourably with older siblings. The effects of racial stereotyping have had consequences too tragic to contemplate – from apartheid against Blacks to genocide against Jews. Hierarchical and class stereotypes have much in common. In the UK a general, a bishop or a judge will often be thought to have middle- or upper-middle-class origins (and this is borne out by statistics), which may not encourage the recruitment of those without.

Let us turn then to group discussion. Here a new element achieves prominence – the oracy of the participants. Of course their prior roles have an influence. An employee may tend to give way to the worse arguments of a managing director in a business meeting. An executive may be concerned to get a policy through a committee by procedural manipulation. An intelligent woman may defer to a silly man on a working party. Nevertheless the possibility exists for another measure of people to operate beyond such status factors – the opportunity to use reason, to appeal to the court of reason.

Roles in group discussion may be described in various ways depending on the purpose of the analysis. An interesting early study by Cornwell classifies them as 'intelligent', 'creative', 'social' (Cornwell 1979: 15–22). Cavanagh and Styles (1987) discern a series of cognitive and interactive roles as Positive and Negative. A common method of analysis is in terms of the nature of the participation: Dominant, Co-operative, Supportive, Acquiescent, Passive, Disruptive. The literature in this area is huge and it is not possible even to begin to consider it here. Instead the next two sections will describe two refreshing investigations. Most studies indicate that females are disadvantaged. One of the interests of Shea's study is that she finds *both* sexes disadvantaged. Robinson's work suggests that roles, defined in cognitive and interactive terms, provide effective criteria for discriminating performances in group discussion.

Sex roles at 7
Gill Shea

'Oh go away you two willies.'

Apart from the obvious physical distinctions the only measurable differences between boys and girls at birth seem to be differences in muscle strength (Sutherland 1981: 70). But then the socialization process is strongly differentiated according to sex. Greif (1980) documents some of the differences between fathers' and mothers' talk with young children – for instance, fathers interrupt more than mothers, and both parents interrupt girls more than boys; fathers try to control conversations more than mothers, and both do so more with girls than with boys. Girls spend more time with their mothers and experience a higher ratio of social to referential speech (speech referring to things) Clark-Stewart 1973 cited in J. Coates 1986: 123). Differentiation also takes place strongly through books, toys and games. The results of this process are observable early. At 2 years 9 months children have more interaction with others of the same sex (Jacklin and Maccoby 1978 cited in Marland 1983) and other studies indicate that 3-year-olds can distinguish toys for boys and for girls. By the age of 4 children differentiate male and female language features with puppet characters.

Notable studies have been carried out on the language of the child and that of the adult and teacher (e.g. Wells 1987) but fewer on the informal interactions of young children. Yet the high number of children per teacher in the early school years suggests that most of their language will be shared with peers, and thus is likely to be as significant in learning as in learning sex roles.

Numerous studies have indicated the apparent superiority of girls in the primary years in tasks demanding verbal ability (Sutherland 1981: 35). But the consensus seems to be that, despite this early linguistic advantage, they are in the long term educationally handicapped. It is suggested that teachers prefer children who are co-operative, quiet and conforming, to those who are active, independent and assertive. Ironically boys suffer the initial handicap of losing the approval of their teacher, but perhaps in the long term they are better able to discover their competencies. Research indicates that boys try to influence what happens in the classroom and they acquire more confidence in their own ability than girls – their motivation to learn comes from themselves rather than desire to please the teacher and they are freer to explore – and learn.

A number of empirical studies confirm that teachers give more attention to boys than girls; it seems that even when teachers are asked to give equal attention to girls and boys they find themselves attending more to the boys. In a detailed description of an infant classroom Paley (in Spender 1982) describes this process and offers some insights into the cause and extent of gender differences.

Language may only be part of the socialization process which leads to sex-differentiated behaviour, but it is a 'vital tool which each of us can use in making sense of the world' (Barnes 1976: 116). In that case we may ask whether boys and girls have equal access to a full set of linguistic tools. Research has concentrated on the educational disadvantages of girls, but it may be that in some ways both sexes are educationally disadvantaged.

A small-scale experiment attempted to explore some of these matters. Groups of four 6–8-year-old children were asked to make a construction from Duplo Lego – a task involving hand and eye which would still permit a free flow of conversation (though it was recognized that building with Lego is not a neutral task). The building task was defined briefly and in very general terms and included the suggestion that children might like to discuss how they were going to organize their activity. The groups were then left with a recorder switched on.

In Group One four boys (5.8–6.1) built a castle. They began building with minimal discussion, and almost immediately began to use a language of personal display. This included the chanting of 'rude' rhymes and phrases such as 'smelly knickers', 'pooh', 'farts' and 'bums'. They seemed to be competing to use the kind of language normally prohibited in the classroom. They also parodied songs, mimicked each other and told jokes. We may conjecture that these were bids for peer approval prompted by the exceptional opportunity to use taboo words in a classroom setting protected by the relative privacy of the sound recorder. Certainly there is evidence of what Paley (1984) describes as the aspirations of the boys to become uncompromisingly aggressive 'superheroes':

John:	Do you know what I can do? I can even get James Campbell over. Is that a good table?
Several voices:	Every one, do you know, do you believe I can get James Campbell over?
Howard:	No.
Nathan:	He can. He runs and jumps on his back, and he falls over, doesn't he? He does.
	(Periods of collective laughter and self-display accompanied the construction of the castle but did not interfere with it)
John:	We haven't got a door.
Nathan:	Is that big enough?
John:	Yeah . . . Yes thanks . . . you can't walk under that, can you Howard?
Howard:	Nah, not really. We're making it higher. That's what we're doing.
Nathan:	I want to put . . .

In spite of occasional enjoinders to 'shut up' there was no apparent ill will or hostility, and little evidence of the hierarchical nature of boys' groups some writers have discerned – Howard appeared to have more prestige, although he spoke less. However, all four used speech to assert dominance, and maintain or assert a claim to the floor.

After about twenty minutes the teacher returned, to see a large, complex and carefully constructed castle, which she asked about. The boys' language changed radically. Each waited for a turn, and expected questions. More interestingly they pointed out features or functions of the castle not discussed in the group, perhaps supplying information they had learnt that teachers expect.

In Group Two four girls (5.7–6.11) were to build a castle for a witch. Unlike the boys they were clearly anxious to fulfil the task requirements, which include the suggestion that they should discuss and plan. They did not begin to build until they had spent approximately fifteen minutes exploring the task and devising possible solutions to practical problems:

> *Ottilie:* Now Leila, before you start making things Mrs Shea said she wanted us to. . . . Did she say she wanted us to . . . ? Design a . . . talk about it . . . right . . . now. Let's just leave the bricks out of the way and now we'll do how many rooms we're going to have and all about it, OK?
>
> *Leila:* We need to have . . .
>
> *Ottilie:* I think we'll need to have one bedroom 'cause the witch would have . . . no she would be . . . she would have her cat on the end of the bed. Do you think so?
>
> (*Agreement*)
>
> Because some people have dogs on the end of their beds.

Most of the discussion centred on finer details of furnishing, such as a cauldron. It was entirely task-oriented, and there were only two minor digressions, neither of which was pursued. When interrupted by the break the girls had used language to plan, to solve problems, and to investigate reality, including the imaginative reality of witches. They listened to each other and rarely interrupted. Disagreement was expressed in tentative terms or in the form of a question.

> *Ottilie:* First we would need a lot of floors.
>
> *Leila:* Well, I know how many?
>
> *Others:* How many?
>
> *Leila:* Six.
>
> *Vivien:* No, 'cause . . .
>
> *Ottilie:* Yes, 'cause some castles are very tall and they do have six, but I don't think we'll be able to do that, Leila. We'll have to have about four.
>
> *Others:* Yeah.

Ottilie, the oldest, was the uncontested leader, and ensured the group planned as instructed, and stayed on task. Her language was like that of a teacher in that although she gave gentle consideration to Leila's suggestion of six floors, she yet ensured her own of four was accepted. Even at this early age these girls use language as Zimmerman says women do: 'Women use minimal responses at points in the conversation which indicate the listener's respect for the current speaker. . . . Their utterances are more tentative because they use forms – hedges – which are less assertive, inviting response, and observing turn-taking' (Zimmerman 1975 cited in J. Coates 1986: 100). The concentration of the girls on language was at the expense of action. After fifteen minutes they had barely begun their building, whereas the boys, who talked more, but for sociability not for the job in hand, had produced a complex edifice.

Group Three, two boys and two girls (5.7–6.1), were concerned to build a school. No consensus appeared in the initial discussion, and the boys became frustrated with talk and demanded action. They soon assumed responsibility for building and the girls played with the remaining Lego. As in the first group the boys alternated their task-oriented language with self-display and fun language. They made noises, used funny voices, and described problems as 'easy peasy for me'. They both constructed the school and entertained the girls who giggled. Girls laugh more with boys than with girls (Haas cited in J. Coates 1986: 131).

Group Four consisted of four boys (7.9–8.1) building a school. As with the younger boys they got on with the task and their conversation was task-oriented talk alternating with social talk, which however contained less self-display and more features to establish group solidarity ('We're the cleverest in the class'), establishing themselves by comparisons with others outside the group, using boasting as a way of building up themselves as group. Individuals no longer shouted each other down but used humour and the strategy of kidding each other to gain agreement. Another feature in both boys' groups was 'intertextuality'. The boys, particularly the older boys, interpolated phrases from Scrooge (their Christmas play), sang songs (often changing the words), parodied television advertisements or programmes. The group acceptance of humour and fun as a strategy, or even a necessity, seemed to encourage them to use metaphors, analogies, parody and irony. These are not the conformist skills that earn approval in the early years of schooling, but there may be links between them and the later educational success of boys.

Group Five consisted of four girls (7.3–7.11) who were building a workshop for Father Christmas; they were similar to the younger group of girls in being almost completely task-oriented. In marked contrast to the boys of similar age (Group Four) they did not feel the need to draw attention to themselves, or to maintain solidarity. They seemed to work together in friendly harmony as individuals:

Catriona: It's getting really good, isn't it?
Hetty: Yes, we're quicker than the boys, aren't we?
Catriona: You never know. One square. . . . Do you mean that the boys are better . . . that we are better than the boys?
Hetty: Yeah, yeah.
Catriona: Well, we're not, are we?
Alice: You never know – they may be quicker than us.

Group Six, of two boys and two girls (7.4–7.8), also built a workshop for Father Christmas. The boys dominated so that the discussion had something of the flavour of an all-boys' group, but here the girls accepted a secondary role less easily. At the end the boys try to make Paula collect the teacher:

Matthew: Who's going to go and get Mrs Shea?
Guy: You are.
Paula: You are
         (*Laughter*)
Paula: I'm not.
Matthew: Yes, you are.
Paula: Oh, go away you two willies.

This study confirms many of the current research findings. The dialogue of girls, even at these early ages, displays many of the characteristics of what we would regard as 'good' group discussion – solving problems by language, listening, supporting, turn-taking, not interrupting, showing courtesy. They perceived the task as work to be done. On the other hand the boys regarded it as 'play' – with reference to home, television and taboo items, not language encouraged in the official curriculum. They used stylized speech events and routines including puns, jokes, irony and humour, not to conform to the teacher's purposes, but to build and maintain a positive self-image which by the age of 8 is subsumed into a strong group cohesion. Girls relate more to authority figures outside the group, such as the teacher from which they may internalize a work ethic. They are anxious to maintain good relationships within the group, but they relate as individuals.

It seems then that not all sexual inequalities in the classroom work in favour of boys. While the boys take risks with language and exploit its range and variety, and use it to explore, this does not seem to give them the freedom to be tentative, to express a variety of feelings, show the concern for justice and empathy with other people, to plan ahead of the event, demonstrated by the girls. In this sense both sexes are linguistically deprived. Attempts to eliminate sexual inequalities will require changes in society, but teachers can initiate change in the classroom, since they have the power to demonstrate what kind of 'reality' is offered. At the moment, to quote Paley, 'Girls tame lions by putting them into houses. Boys conquer houses by sending them into space' (Paley 1984: 9).

Positive and negative roles (13–15)
Geoffrey Robinson

Yes, but that depends . . .

To investigate their roles in discussion small groups of pupils at 13 and at 15 were recorded on two topics, one of which, 'What would you like to change about your school?', is considered here. There were two boys and two girls in each group, chosen not so much for their apparent academic ability, as for their ability to articulate their thoughts, and their willingness to discuss (Robinson 1988).

Work done in Canada by Cavanagh and Styles (1987) seeks to utilize positiveness in group discussion by encouraging pupils to adopt 'helpful' roles as distinct from 'hindering' ones. Drawing on this work, on that of Berrill (1988) and also on personal observation, an instrument was devised taking into account the need to assess 'process' as well as 'product'. It categorized roles under Interactive Skills (I) and under Cognitive Skills (C), Positive (P) and Negative (N). Here is the system as revised as a result of the investigation:

Roles taken in group work

Positive roles	Negative roles

Interactive Skills

Positive roles	Negative roles
1 Encourages others to make a contribution	Discourages others from making a contribution
2 Organizes well	Fragments the discussion
3 Persuades well	Acquiesces too readily
4 Challenges in a positive and mature way	Fails to challenge even glaringly wrong statements or challenges indiscriminately
5 Monitors/responds to needs of listeners	Fails to understand/adapt to listeners' needs
6 Is confident	Badly under-confident or over-dominant
7 Puts group needs high	Self comes first
8 Co-operates with others	Disrupts
9 Negotiates, helps define and re-define roles in the group	Unaware of his/her or others' roles in the group
10 Tension relieving: uses humour in a positive way	Clowning: messes around and jokes at others' expense.
11 Mediates/negotiates well	Lacks diplomacy, provokes others in disputes
12 Chairperson moves: co-ordinates discussion, keeps group to tasks and agenda	No attempt to keep to tasks and agenda
13 Uses paralinguistic features to show attentiveness and response when listening and to enhance speech when talking	If any paralinguistic features present at all they indicate inattentiveness and lack of response when listening and detract from the message when talking
14 Shows knowledge of the 'rules' of turn-taking and applies them	Lacks understanding of the 'rules' and courtesies of conversation
15 Can sustain a longer turn and maintain utterance, even when threatened with interruption	Can only sustain short turns and is too ready to back down when threatened with interruption
16 Exploits turn-taking intelligently/sensitively, e.g. sets up adjacency pairings; uses Socratic questioning, etc.	Unable to make turn-taking work for him/her

Cognitive Skills

Positive roles	Negative roles
1 Readily introduces ideas	Few ideas forthcoming
2 Reasons, argues or concedes a case intelligently	Reasons poorly, uses arguments of dubious validity or argues belligerently,

Positive roles	Negative roles
	never conceding a case even when obviously wrong
3 Responds to others' ideas: supports, builds on, modifies, challenges, etc.	Fails to respond to others' ideas: ignores, changes topic, etc.
4 Analyses/evaluates	Trivializes/responds superficially
5 Hypothesizes	Fails to think in abstractions
6 Explains and elaborates well	Confuses matters
7 Asks questions which seek information, challenge, move discussion on, etc.	Asks few questions. When he does they are irrelevant, poorly framed, have already been answered
8 Uses anecdote or illustration to illuminate topic	If uses anecdote or illustration at all, irrelevant or unilluminating
9 Summarizes	Signs of having failed to assimilate group ideas

In the analyses which follows 'C' indicates Cognitive, 'I' Interactive, 'P' Positive, and 'N' Negative. Thus 'C.3P.' indicates the third Positive role in the Cognitive area.

The 13-year-olds freely introduced ideas into the discussion but there was a tendency for them not to be developed very fully either by the initiator or by others. While supporting and adding, they were less likely to evaluate, analyse, challenge in any significant way one another's contributions (C.3,4P.). Probably this accounts for the more frequent change of topic than with the 15-year-olds. Let us compare a passage of conversation from each group.

After an initial burst of ideas the 13-year-olds flounder, and digress on the recent maths examination. This brings the first 'chairing' move from Noel (I.12P.), who pulls them back to the topic:

Noel: I'd like to change the opening times for the library so you can get books.
Edward: Yeah, you expect it to be open at lunch times and . . .
Kate: That is open at lunch times but I want dinner.
Edward: Break time then.
Noel: I wouldn't mind it in the morning, 'cause I don't mind . . .
Edward: Yeah.
Noel: . . . fishing books. Can't be bothered . . .
Kate: And after school.
Noel: . . . getting them at break time.
Edward: Well it's open after school, but not long enough really.

Noel's chairing move (the first of a number he makes) is executed diplomatically (I.11P.). Edward's attempt to support him is not well informed, but shows attention to and support of others (C.3P.), a role he frequently takes. Kate's correction of Edward's point is joined with her further back up of Noel's proposal for a change of times. There follows Noel's argument for mornings because he can't be bothered to go after school (C.2N.), egocentrical rather than logical.

Finally Edward's constructive modification of Kate's erroneous statement demonstrates a diplomatic role (I.11,12P.). Contrast Kate's contradiction of Edward in the third utterance of the interchange.

The 15-year-olds return to the topic of school uniform they have already touched upon. Sanjit now sounds out a hypothesis on how rules on uniform could be made to work.

Sanjit: Yeah but if you have a strict uniform like you've got to wear these kinds of trousers, any one can wear any kind . . .

Jane: Yeah.

Sanjit: . . . of trousers – pleated, turn-ups.

Jane: Easier, say like, yeah . . .

Sanjit: Anything, but if you have a strict one say like you've got to get these kind then it will work then.

Jane: Yeah.

Colin: I don't think it will work.

Katie: Because a . . .

Colin: Whatever uniform you have people will abuse it.

Sanjit: Yes, but that depends on how strict you're going to be.

Katie: People like just breaking rules.

Jane: Yeah.

Katie: Don't they?

There are a number of elements in this series which enable the participants to achieve this quality of discourse. First, Sanjit attempts a hypothesis to answer the problems of school uniform raised by others (C.5P.). He builds his argument effectively (C.2P.) and elaborates his point (C.6P.) to produce a persuasive piece of speech (I.3P.). Jane's supportive monitoring encourages a number of speakers in their contributions, even when their views differ from hers (prior to this section she had disagreed with Sanjit on the issue). Her involvement in the discussion is clear from her responses which she attempts to elaborate in the fourth utterance, but sadly she is not able to continue. Her role might well receive little attention or merit in many schemes of oral assessment but in this she makes a positive role contribution (C.3P. and I.1P. – encouraging others).

The 13-year-olds on the whole are supportive of one another, and challenge is on the level of fact. More strenuous challenge elsewhere in the discussion can cause them to become abusive ('Close the tuck shop? Don't be stupid!'). On the other hand the 15-year-olds can challenge more sharply and on the level of ideas and keep the discussion impersonal.

It is not possible to consider all the roles in detail. With the 13-year-olds the full range of Cognitive Skills can be found but may operate on a comparatively superficial level. Most of this group had still to develop the ability to discuss issues from different viewpoints. There tended to be fewer Interactive Skills in evidence than with the 15-year-olds, although those that did appear (Noel's 'chairing' for example – I.12P.) were impressive, and members of the group showed confidence in their contributions (I.6P.) and co-operation (I.7P.). However they tended to speak less persuasively (I.3N.), and could (as we have seen) resort to abuse at an unpopular point.

With the 15-year-olds the topics they considered tended to be more sustained with group members not only introducing ideas but also developing their cases and arguing them through. It is not surprising, therefore, that we see more long turns. Participants are more likely to modify and challenge, truly engage with the previous turn, and often presenting a new perspective or a different viewpoint. Arguments attain a greater depth, showing an understanding and knowledge over and above that of the 13-year-olds whose experiences of life are more limited. The 15-year-olds tend to be more analytical of topics and of one another's arguments.

Now it's my turn

We learn the rules to play the game; we play the roles to make our contribution to it. Ideally we should be able to play a range of roles – from the glittering lead to that of the pudding who says nothing until his or her final clinching intervention. These are the kinds of roles discussed by Geoffrey Robinson – they can be used to positive or negative effect. The other kind of role is that which the person has or plays irrespective of the discussion, as for instance a sex role, as in Gill Shea's contribution (pp. 79–83). Awareness of such roles as a step towards dealing with their negative aspects is one of the motives behind the devising of self-assessment schedules which are figuring increasingly in oral evaluation (e.g. Cavanagh and Styles 1987; Robinson 1988; British Columbia Student Assessment 1988; Mowbray 1987).

The Cox Report is aware of the importance of role. Level 9.ii requires pupils to have 'an active part on group discussions, displaying sensitivity, listening critically, e.g. to attempts to persuade, and being self-critical' (DES 1989: 15.24). The expectation for Level 9 would be that the pupils would be in their mid-teens. Our researches reported in this book suggest that some children of 7 may be described as having these abilities. Wherein then lie the differences between the rule and role operations of children at different levels? This is a question addressed in the previous section, and one which we shall consider further in the next part of the book.

PART THREE

English is there: aspects of language awareness

English is there, in use all the time, by different groups, in a variety of situations. Let us show children what there is: and, showing them, help them to a wider control and a greater tolerance over other registers, other styles. And let our description and production deal with the real facts of the real language.

What is language? Three types of answers seem relevant: language is behaviour; language is skill; language is speech. Let us take each of these in turn.

First, language is a system of behaviour. By system of behaviour we mean that it is not arbitrary, it conforms, it shows order; it is, in fact, patterned: it consists of patterns, phonological (or containing sounds), grammatical, and lexical (or made up of vocabulary items); we might surmise too that there are contextual patterns but this is still an area of great uncertainty. Like all behaviour systems, then, language is patterned; equally like all such systems it takes place in time and it must be learned. No child is born talking but every normal child is born capable of learning one language, fluently, as it were: this one language can, of course, be *any* language; a Chinese child brought up from birth in England by English speakers learns English as a native speaker and has as much difficulty later on in learning Chinese as any English child. Some people might want to add that, like other behaviour, all speech is made in response to the speaker's situation (or stimulus), what arises from other speakers' utterances, or, if his is the initial utterance, what stimulates in the situation itself. Others might want to bring in ideas of purpose and heredity but it is doubtful if such ideas make the explanations any more powerful. The patterning of language must not seduce us into thinking about *rules*: the patterning of an individual language is both purely conventional, and purely arbitrary: conventional within itself (but permanently changing); arbitrary in relation to other languages (there is no *reason*, in logic or anything else, for the English statement order to be: *Tom is in the house* than for the normal Welsh statement order to be: *Mae Tom yn y ty*, i.e. *Is Tom in the house*).

Second, language is a skill used in communication. This has two almost conflicting implications: first, that all do not possess the same amount of skill, second, that all have enough for their own needs. It is common sense that people's language skill (and we speak always of their first language) differs. There is, as it were, within the language corpus a set of patterns which, in the total sense, are finite but for the individual speaker are infinite: in other words no speakers ever learn all the possible patterns of their language. But at the same time all speakers perform adequately within their own range of patterns. We might think of walking as a comparable (though much simpler) behaviour system. Some people walk faster (and so on) than others but they do not, unless they are tired, run out of walking patterns (or, in this case, movements). And all walkers walk adequately for their own needs. Similarly, all normal people speak adequately for their own needs within their own immediate environment. They may, of course, be illiterate but then literacy is a rather late and highly specialized development. Every language that is known is spoken; not all are written, though, of course, all could be. Only the educated speak and write; all (normally) speak their own mother tongue.

And so to the third type of answer: language is speech. Spoken language (unless a contrast is intended with listening, what the listener hears) is a tautology: there is language and there is written language. Language, if you like, is the unmarked member of the pair; or, more simply, speech is somehow more the real language and writing is always some sort of representation of speech.

(Davies in Wilkinson 1965: 38 and 19–20)

10 The study of language

ALAN DAVIES

The spoken language and the written language

There is need for a proper balance in language and language teaching as in other areas of life. In language that balance is between stability and change. Both are necessary. Stability makes communication both possible and efficient, across space (between speakers of different dialects) and across time (between different generations). Without stability language would die because it would be too personal, totally individual. Change allows language to accommodate itself to new ideas and needs. Without change language would die because it would be wholly social (and only at one time period) and not reflect the individual and the personal at all. Stability is the social push, change the individual. It would be easy to suggest that it is change that is normal (what linguists call the unmarked form, in computer language the default mode, what happens naturally) and stability the unusual, the mode that must be specially arranged. This is not the case. They reflect different aspects of human learning and behaviour, change the individual/ psychological and stability the social. Society is made up of individuals; individuals form themselves into societies. Both need what the other has. Human beings are both individual and social; for communities to survive and develop both stability and change must be in harmony: so with language.

Individuals bring their own language/idiolect and map it on to the language (code) of their society. The individual's potential for creative change is to some extent related to the role of the Spoken Language since it is that medium which contains the largest range of innovations, the slang, the jargon, the coinages and the borrowings which mark (and identify) successive generations. In spite of individual creative manipulation, it is membership of groups (social, geographic and so on) rather than individuals that the spoken language particularly identifies. That is true. Nevertheless, it is above all in the *spoken* language where speakers practise their creativity (except of course in the few cases of creative writers). The spoken language is fugitive, both as a record of what we have just said/heard, and as a data base for the language, perhaps for the same reason, in that we retain no account of what has been said, and indeed, forget most of it. So for the sake of keeping a written record of what has been spoken, as much as for the need to retell what has been said to some interlocutor not present on the first occasion – to fulfil that need some agreement on how to record (in writing), how to repeat (in speaking) and indeed how to think about it (in thinking) is needed. The spoken language must have stability in addition to its facility for change. The same can be said for the written language.

The written language maintains contact over time and space; as such, as we shall see, it tends to be the language of the educated classes and therefore the medium of the standard language. Through needed conformity the written language also acts as a norm of what it is we are trying to say; in that sense the written language *is* the language while the spoken language is the idiolect. And yet the written language also needs to admit change in order to make it possible for science, journalism, literature and so on to reflect social changes. It is interesting to note that the two areas of the written language which seem most resistant to this change we have insisted it must admit are law and religion, the two areas which are probably, indeed necessarily, those which bear the stability of any society. For law and religion (and therefore their language medium) to change, signals a more basic change in society, than a cultural and restorable change through the sciences and literature. There is of course a counter-argument, challenging this lesser and separate role given to science and literature. We shall not pursue it here but it is an issue which comes up regularly in discussions of new translations of the Bible, of the status of the Koran and therefore of the principle of censorship, as demonstrated in recent years in television (the Mary Whitehouse and Moral Majority campaigns), in film (*The Last Temptation of Christ*) and in the novel (*The Satanic Verses*). This question is for another occasion but it is well to reflect that such questions are relevant to our consideration of the spoken and the written language.

We can represent our discussion thus far in a simple form:

Change	Individual	Spoken Language	Dialect
Stability	Society	Written Language	Standard language

Public statements about language usually take it for granted that we know what language is. Whether these statements come as reactions to reports on the teaching of English, on reading standards, on the need for modern language skills after 1992, or more generally as comments in letters in the public prints on language standards and language change, all represent a similar view. This view has to do with norms, with standards, with correctness. The tone is one of regret and loss of a better, richer, truer language. This is the mythic view of language change, a view also found in other areas of social life, looking back romantically to a prelapsarian state of near perfection, a time when Shakespeare was writing plays, Dr Johnson prose, Dickens and Austen novels. There are two replies to this complaint (in reality there is no answer!) – first, that language change is inevitable, like it or not; second, that today's language both benefits from earlier writers and has plenty of creative writers whose works will last. (We will come back to the question of correctness and the standard language.)

This is not of course a new view. The Tracts of the Society for Pure English through the 1920s and 1930s were full of it and in the eighteenth century Robert Lowth wrote in his *Short Introduction to English Grammar* (1762) 'that the English Language as it is spoken by the politest part of the nation, and as it stands in the writing of our most approved authors, often offends against every part of Grammar'. Such a view would be preposterous were it not actually quite common. It is difficult to see what Lowth meant by an error unless it was something that offended against the divine. One explanation for this false view of a fixed language (making language into a permanent text) is the way language is often observed. We are here describing the lay view and it is only fair to remark that lay views of complex subjects are typically naive. In most instances however lay people recognize their naivety because they know they don't know. But language is different. Because it is so close to everyone we like to think we can understand it all. Such lay views are often expressed in normative and legalistic ways.

The correctness view of language is that it is made up of sentences and words and that these are fixed in how they are organized, in their meanings and in their pronunciation. It is largely because such views are held so passionately that strong feelings are expressed about the slovenliness of contemporary speech and the illiteracy of reading and writing in today's schools. It also explains reactions to the recent Kingman Report (DES 1988a) and Cox Reports (DES 1988b; 1989) on the teaching of English in schools. Cox is no latter-day Lowth. He has accepted linguistic ideas about language change and language systems but has also recognized the importance of a conventional or social norm. Hence the realistic placing of Standard English as one dialect among many and yet, at the same time, the one most desirable for school use on the grounds that it is the one most widely known and used nationally (especially in writing) and internationally.

Inevitably Cox comes under attack from two quarters. On the one hand he is attacked because he is not liberal enough, because he admits and values local dialects and uses. That line is attacked because it opens the gates to illiteracy and chaos (for example Honey 1983). On the other hand he is attacked by the more radical teachers' groups for being over-normative since that is a denial of the child's development through his or her own language. We are constantly being told that unless children are allowed to make use of their home language (or dialect, the argument is the same) for education their cognitive development, perhaps their emotional development also, will suffer. And so the Cox Committee is criticized for being over-prescriptive, for insisting on the Standard Language and for apparently advocating the teaching of formal grammar (a very loaded key indicator for the progressives). As a result he must tread the narrow line between progressives and reactionaries.

Linguistic views of language

Cox has, in spite of his conservatism (for which we have praised him) made a huge leap forward from Lowth. That leap in part shows the influence of linguistics (see for example Yule 1985). Twentieth-century linguistics, building on Saussure and Bloomfield, and Jespersen has had an influence in the intellectual community; its influence elsewhere has been less wide. What linguistics says about language is that the correctness views of sentences, words and pronunciations need modification.

Basically language is not content but form. That is the fundamental structuralist argument put forward by Saussure. As such form must adapt to changing content. Of the three categories – sentences, words and pronunciation – which are regarded as fixed the second (words) and third (pronunciation) are indeed very changeable as historical dictionaries show for word meanings and old texts such as plays and poems indicate for pronunciation (through rhyming evidence). Sentences change less in the sense that the structure of an English sentence is less open to innovation. Even so sentences are open to change from three quarters:

1 There are many alternative sentence patterns in English.
2 The errors so often complained about are not so much structural ones as dialectal differences and therefore stigmatized in favour of standard language forms (for example '*We was . . .*') or standard language options indicating perhaps change of convention (for example the split infinitive, or *due to/owing to*).
3 The sentences that are appealed to are those of the written language, not of the spoken language. It is a truism that sentences are what are written and utterances are what are spoken. The spoken language is not made up of well-formed sentences such as we expect to find in the written language. As we shall see it is useful to make a distinction between *system sentences* and *text sentences* (Lyons 1977) which allow us to explain that the incoherence of the spoken language is normal. What often appear to be incoherent, half-finished, elliptical or even slovenly spoken language utterances do in fact depend on and can be systematically related to *system sentences*. In other words, underlying the spoken language is the same system or set of systems as that underlying the written language. The system(s) is just more obvious in the written language.

There are other lay views about language acquisition and about the relation of language and thought. What linguistics has helped do in both cases is to suggest that language can be seen as a tool. Its acquisition comes with use rather than with being told about it (at least in the First Language 1 situation). Its relation to thought is just not straightforward. For some people there may be a close relation but this is not generally the case and is never necessarily so. Language gives us a medium for thinking but it is not thought itself, nor need it constrain our thinking unless we want it to. The strong linguistic relativity position maintains that we are at the mercy of our language in our thinking. We see the world in terms of our language categories. This is a view associated with Sapir (1960) and Whorf (1956). It is generally felt to be over-stated. While language does influence us, so that for example I label colours in terms of my First Language 1, that does not prevent me from perceiving other shades and hues.

The problem (apart from a philosophical one) with this Sapir–Whorf strong view is that it would not allow translation or second language learning to take place. They may not take place perfectly but common sense tells us that they do take place.

The focus of linguistic study has always been microlinguistic, that is on the central language systems. These concern the ways in which sounds and meanings are connected and deal therefore with sound systems (phonology), meaning systems (semantics) and sentence systems (grammar). Attached to these central systems are a number of related systems, phonetics (the general study of the speech mechanisms), lexis (the study of vocabulary systems) and pragmatics (the mapping of what is said on to what is meant). In addition grammar is often subdivided into syntax, dealing solely with sentences, and morphology which concerns 'word formations'.

The emphasis in microlinguistics in the 1960s has been extended in more recent years by extensive work in various macrolinguistic areas, notably in the study of systems beyond/above the sentence, work under headings such as discourse analysis, text linguistics, and conversation analysis, as well as developments in the bracketed areas of linguistics with other systems, notably psycholinguistics, sociolinguistics and of course cognitive science with the important place given to linguistic systems in artificial intelligence and computer technology. The two areas of most interest to the spoken language, discourse analysis and conversation analysis reflect different starting positions. On the whole discourse analysis is the approach from linguistics into sentence relationships while conversation analysis is the approach to some of the same phenomena but from a starting-point in for example sociology or education. There is a more distant interest (shown for example in ethnomethodology) into conversation but with a focus on what the data mean for social structures and relations and not for language.

What has happened therefore in the last twenty years, curiously, is an apparent turn-round, a return to a concentration on the spoken language. The modern period of linguistics study can be characterized by a move in focus of interest from the spoken language to the written language and now back again to the spoken language.

This can best be explained I suggest as a reflection of the interaction between two very different traditions, the one more anthropological and sociolinguistic (hence the interest in speech), the other more linguistic and psycholinguistic (hence the interest in the written language). The first is more open to variation and interaction, the second more accepting of a context-free syntax. The fact is that each needs the other, neither is complete. Language is all these things:

concentration on one side, on *language in use* (not itself identical with the spoken language but most easily discussed as if it were the spoken language) leads to a surfeit of information since in the *language in use* situation (such as the spoken language interaction) so much is going on at the same time that it is difficult to study and analyse. Equally concentration on the *language rule* side (again not itself the written language though as we have seen it looks more like the written language) leads again to a sense of frustration that not *enough* information is being investigated for us to understand how language works.

Two examples are intonation and accent: written language texts (obviously) do not show intonation (nor incidentally do written transcripts of spoken language texts), nor do they (normally) show accent. Both intonation and accent are important aspects of the spoken language. Are they however important aspects of *language*?

There are three answers to this.

1 The written language has other ways (for example adverbs, orthography) of showing intonation and accent.
2 Except in literature the written language functions differently from the spoken language and is unlikely to need to capture intonation and accent.
3 Forcing the argument to: 'it depends on what you mean by *the language*' compels an unsatisfactory choice between the written language and the spoken language. That is an unnecessary and self-defeating choice to have to make. Much better to admit that *both* are the language, that of course underlying *both* the written language (and only apparently isomorphic to it) *and* the spoken language is a set of syntactical rules, and equally of course these rules operate as choices in relation to other sets of rules in relevant situations, such as intonation, accent, style and genre.

We have suggested ways of looking at the spoken language and the written language. But what is language? Four types of answers seem relevant: language is behaviour; language is knowledge; language is skill; language is speech. Let us take these in turn.

First, language is a system of behaviour. By 'system of behaviour' we mean that it is not arbitrary, it conforms, it shows order; it is, in fact, patterned: it consists of patterns, phonological, grammatical and lexical and so on. As we have seen, it also consists of discourse patterns although these are more difficult to be precise about. Like all behaviour systems, then, language is patterned; equally like all such systems it takes place in time and must be learned. No child is born talking but every normal child is born capable of learning one language fluently, as it were. This one language can be any language: a Chinese child brought up by birth in the UK by English-speaking parents learns English as a native speaker and has as much difficulty later on learning Chinese as any other British child. The patterning of language must not seduce us into thinking about rules: the patterning of an individual language is both purely conventional and purely arbitrary, conventional within itself (but permanently changing); arbitrary in relation to other languages (there is no reason in logic for the English declarative statement order to be *Tom is in the house* than for the normal Welsh order to be *Mae Tom yn y ty*, that is, *Is Tom in the house*).

Second, language is knowledge. Language relates to other knowledge systems such as science for which we use language to discuss, describe and so on. But more than that language is knowledge in itself. This is obvious for not only the content aspect of language (meanings, their reference to the world and to one another) but also the form aspect of language because of the role of language in thinking. Furthermore there is an aspect of language which allows us to know about language itself, the so-called metalinguistic function which allows us for example to talk about language using grammatical terminology.

Third, language is skill used in communication. This has two almost conflicting implications: first that all do not possess the same amount of skill, second that all have enough for their own needs. It is common observation that individuals differ in their language skills; we speak here of *first* language skills, and it is even more obvious for *second/foreign* language skills. There is as it were within the language corpus a set of patterns which are finite but for the individual speaker are infinite. In other words no speakers ever learn all the possible patterns of their language. But at the same time all speakers perform adequately within their own range of patterns. We might think by analogy of *walking* as a comparable behaviour system. Some people walk faster than others but they do not, unless they are tired, run out of walking patterns (or, in this case, movements). And all walkers walk adequately for their own needs. Similarly all normal people speak adequately for their own needs within their own immediate environment. They may be illiterate but that is a contingent factor since literacy is a late and highly specialized development. Every language that is known is spoken; not all are written, though of course all could be. Only the educated speak and write; all individuals (normally) speak their own mother tongue.

Fourth, language is speech. As we have just indicated, speech is always prior, prior in the life of the individual (ontogenetically) and prior in the life of societies (phylogenetically). In spite of our strong view on the differential functions of speech and writing, nevertheless speech is more the language than writing is, if only because it is always possible to speak what has been written but impossible to find any mode of writing that will convey all the parameters of speech. Variation among individuals and groups (such as Americans and British or Cockneys and Cornish) is found much more markedly in speech than in writing.

We have agreed that both the written language and the spoken language are fundamentally the same language; it is also clear that they each make/choose different selections of linguistic (etc.) features appropriate to the functions they are fulfilling. It is further clear that within the spoken language and the written language continuum there is a substantial overlap where we have on the one hand a *written type of spoken language* (speaking like a book) which can be more written language or more spoken language so that reading aloud a written report is very much on the written language side, while acting a play, speaking the lines, is more

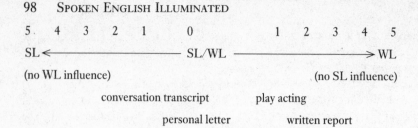

Figure 1   Continuum of spoken or written language

on the spoken language side. On the other hand we have a *spoken type of written language* which again can be more spoken language or more written language so that a written transcript of a conversation is more on the spoken language side while a very informal personal letter might be more on the written language side. We have a continuum as shown in Figure 1. Each modality has difficulty in incorporating the features of the other. As we have suggested this does not matter as long as each is concerned with its own function and is not attempting to represent the other. The written language does not need intonation, it either has alternative features (for example adverbs) or it does not seek to indicate those meanings conveyed by intonation. Similarly the spoken language does not need physical substance to provide a memorial since it contains generous redundancy, notably repetition, to take the place of a physical external memory, as in a written text. So far so good. There is a major problem however when the one modality attempts to convey those features of the other it lacks: when the written language wishes to show precisely intonation (as in a play) there are various metalinguistic routines that can be used. Or when the spoken language wishes to convey the logical argumentation of the written language this can be difficult because the density of written argument is not easy to present in speech.

Most difficult of all is the problem that the spoken language gives to self-representation and thereby reflection for all those who wish to reflect and analyse. In addition there are no agreed conventions on how to record the spoken language in writing, as there are of course for the written language, one excellent indication of the need for a standard language. The problem is that any written representation of the spoken language is by definition a misrepresentation because it necessarily involves some form of idealization, some adjustment of what was said in terms of available (and standard) orthographies, and so on. The same problem is not acute for the written language's own record of itself since it is, again by definition, a modality of record. Brown and Yule (1983) give some useful examples of the problem of capturing the spoken language.

Dialect, accent, register, style

In addition to linguistic levels and categories we can also approach language in terms of dialect, accent, register and style.

First, dialect and accent. The separation between the two is often blurred but it is useful to keep them apart. Dialect is more a matter of grammar and vocabulary; accent of pronunciation. Different dialects usually have different accents. What makes British and American English different is partly dialectal and partly accentual. There are well-known vocabulary differences (for example, boot–trunk; college–school) as well as grammatical ones (How many do you have? How many have you got?). In the UK there are similar dialectal differences (between for example Scotland and the south of England) but perhaps because of the strong social class structure it is accent differences that arouse most interest.

Second, register. Here we are dealing with the varieties of English used by occupational groups and these tend to be part grammatical but mainly lexical and hardly at all phonological. We assume that professional groups use a special form of English. There is a tendency to object to such jargons and yet it is surely part of learning how to be a lawyer, doctor, sailor, scientist, accountant, engineer and so on to become accustomed to the ways in which they normally talk in the conduct of their work, and then to talk that way ourselves as we learn to become members of that profession. The development in recent years of English for Specific Purpose (mainly concerned with the teaching of English as a Foreign Language) indicates the great range of special uses of the language. When engineers wish to describe (in writing) the way in which a turbine starts they might begin: 'the starting of the turbine is effected by rotation of a handwheel' (Herbert 1965). The non-engineer (or the engineer when speaking perhaps) might write 'the turbine is started by turning a handwheel'. The important point here is the combining of the word *effected* with the passive voice. There is little point in asking why engineers do this. Specific purpose language is no more (or less) logical than language itself. The point is that this is the way it is done.

Third, style. Dialect, accent and register divide language users on historical or biographical principles. You speak like this because you come from . . . , because you belong to. . . . Style divides according to situation and appropriateness. A long-established systematization proposed by Joos (1962) is still illuminating. Joss suggests a Style Scale with five ranks: frozen, formal, consultative, casual, intimate. Let us attempt an example by saying the same thing at each rank of the scale and then look more closely. In each case it is the situation that changes. This probably implies a change of person addressed, that is a change of relation. But within two or three ranks of the scale it might simply imply a change of attitude to the same person. Thus these five ways of asking the time might be suggested:

1 Frozen   I should be glad to be informed of the correct time.
2 Formal   I should like to know the time, please.
3 Consultative Do you have the time on you, please?
4 Casual   What's the time?
5 Intimate   Time?

This example does not ring true and cannot because the constraints imposed on us by situation direct us not only towards attitude and relationship but also to the content of what we say. Thus in the example, (1) is impossible and (2) unlikely.

The formal style is reserved for addressing strangers or for getting over the barrier of formality (as in lectures). True you might ask complete strangers in the street for the time but you would be likely to impose on them a lower (more personal) rank of style, say consultative, because of the very urgency of your request. And the frozen style is reserved entirely for writing. The example (1) given here is in effect a highly formal one. The point of there being a rank higher than formal simply means that here we go into communication through writing.

To Joos it is the consultative style that is the norm of spoken English. This is the style we generally use for coming to terms with strangers or for speaking to colleagues, friends and so on, when there is some important information to convey. In Text 1 below the two speakers are colleagues, well known to one another, but since they are trying to work out a difficult conceptual problem it is the consultative rather than the casual style that is employed. The two main characteristics of the consultative style are the supply of background information which the listener does not know and the continuous participation of the listener (indicated in Text 1 by the listener code markers such as 'yes' and the change-over when listener becomes speaker).

In the casual style it is still public information which holds the centre of attention (otherwise the speakers lapse into jokes or silence: Tannen and Saville-Troike 1985). The participants are friends, members of a primary group. Its characteristics are ellipsis or abbreviation (for examples 'have two lots of' instead of 'well the thing to do is to have two lots of') and slang. Slang is ephemeral, its use restricted to the casual style where it marks inclusion within and acceptance by the social group. For the intimate style Joos has the defining characteristics of extraction and jargon. Extraction refers to reduced indicators of routines that are well rehearsed between two people who are very close (members of a family, husband and wife, and so on). A nod, smile, look, one word can trigger off a whole meaning. That is extraction. Jargon in the intimate style may be fossilized slang but unlike slang it is permanent and has significance only for members of the intimate group. There are familial terms which have meaning only for that family.

In each of these three styles there is constant and immediate listener participation. In the other two there is none. In the formal style (Joos defines this style as having detachment and cohesion) there is information to convey. This is the style of the lecturer or public speaker, of formal introductions and greetings. The material is prepared beforehand. Public speakers whose material is badly organized find themselves slipping, to the unexpected embarrassment of their audience into the consultative style without the necessary audience reinforcement essential to that style. The frozen style is the style of writing, or, Joos says, of declamation. A simple way of distinguishing frozen and formal might be to think of a lecture read from a printed paper which has been written for publication and a lecture read from fairly full notes or from a text, fully written out but designed for speaking aloud. Hence the apologies in published collections of lectures for their lack of frozenness.

11 The spoken language

ALAN DAVIES

Features of the spoken language

We turn now to a close examination of some features of the spoken language, using two very different spoken language texts for discussion. Then we compare a third spoken language text with a matching written language text in order to illustrate the differences between the two modalities. We then return to the written language and consider the functions it is said best to fulfil. Finally, we relate the spoken language and the written language together and consider a reconciliation in terms of the twin claims of oracy and literacy.

The first text is a transcription in graphic script of a discussion recorded between two educational psychologists. It is in the consultative style. (The second speaker's remarks are italicized.)

Text 1

 1 a streamed school um will have a particular kind of headmaster
 2 broadly speaking . . . and he will tend to employ a particular
 3 kind of staff . . . the whole thing is built in in interactions . . .
 4 this is why . . . I'm saying *do we know that though I mean or is*
 5 *that just an assumption we're making . . . in fact* well . . . um . . .
 6 I think I could quote a number of studies here not many where
 7 where this is known um study of physical education where we're
 8 trying to compare or they were trying to compare children
 9 who'd been trained by movement training PT people . . . and
10 people trained in the traditional PT way . . . but the whole
11 atmosphere of the school reinforced the effects of these two
12 because the three movement trained . . . teachers were in what
13 you would regard even if you didn't though know noth nothing
14 about their physical education . . . and now there more or less
15 um . . . um democratic child-centred schools . . . I don't know
16 how what words words to put in here . . . that the three tradi-

17 tional PT people belonged to three schools you've described
18 without knowing thing about the PT as traditional authori-
19 tarian . . . schools . . . [We cut the text here and take up the
20 speaker at a later point.]
21 I'd start by saying that the primary variable in in the school is
22 teacher personality her view of . . . children her view of her role
23 and things of that sort *mm* the only thing about the structure of
24 the school I would take into account is er well the first form
25 would be size of class . . . in relation but not second form the
26 view the teacher has of what children are and what her role is
27 and so on . . . I wouldn't start with gross features of education
28 like er the structure of the school I think I'd make that subsi-
29 diary to what goes on in the classroom so I'd start with teacher
30 personality *but then you're making you're making an assumption*
31 that's my assumption yes *well the thing to do is to have two lots*
32 *of research going on one working on your assumption* mm *and one*
33 *working from the structural structure of the school assumption* yes
34 *and to see um which would give you now which would you regard*
35 *as the most the better experiment the one that brings you what* in
36 consequences of *mm* of findings *yes what* the right *yes what yes*
37 *of findings and which* will exams be able to explain the structure
38 of the school er er er my view my start would be better than
39 the start taking the structure of the school as given because I
40 would be able to explain why the structure of the school has
41 arisen *no you might simply be explaining why that sort of*
42 *teachers are in the next school because that that type of personality*
43 *may be attracted by that structure in fact I think that's what*
44 *happens isn't it* I agree with you yes *really so it's er a chicken and*
45 *egg argument* but the other argument

Text 1 contains several common features of everyone's speech which we often
ignore or are embarrassed about because we tend to think of the spoken language
in written terms. There are

1 gaps (indicated by dots); here the speakers pause while they think: this is
   obvious but is not always indicated in written conversation (for example in
   novels);
2 hesitations (*er* line 38; *um* line 1; half-begun words such as *noth* line 13);
3 stabilizers (*I mean* line 4; *in fact* line 5; *well* line 24; *yes* line 36);
4 listener code markers (*yes* line 33; *mm* line 23);
5 initial markers (*well* line 31; *but* line 30);
6 repetitions (*you're making you're making* line 30; *that that*, line 42);
7 renewals (*which would give you now which would you regard* line 34; *as the most the*
   better line 35);
8 anacoluthon (possibly lines 10–15).

But it is highly significant that in such an intense consultative situation, although there are no sentences to literate eyes, the total structure never really breaks down (for example first paragraph). The speaker finishes a grammatical pattern (except when interrupted by a colleague whose very interruptions – *mm, yes* – are themselves part of the total grammar and, of course, part of the consultative style), finishes it and lapses into silence or immediately starts another pattern.

Several of the features may be subsumed under the heading of redundancy, the transmission of superfluous information, which we see at its most obvious in the simple lexical repetitions and in the grammatical renewals in the text. But the listener code markers, indicative of addressee participation, also convey no additional information (something needs to be done to show that the listener is listening but what is being said by the listener is irrelevant and some non-linguistic code such as a smile, nod, and so on could be used).

Text 2 is a transcription of a tape 1 made some years ago during a family breakfast, the chief purpose being to compare so-called natural data with supposedly similar data in language teaching materials. The tape used for the analysis was the outcome of a number of practices with the recording equipment to accustom the family to its presence. An account of the subsequent comparison can be found in Davies (1978). Here we are primarily concerned with the spoken language features represented in this text.

Text 2 (Davies family breakfast)

Orthographic words are used in this transcription. There is no punctuation. Dots indicate pauses, with some attempt to show length. Question marks indicate lack of tape clarity. Words in parentheses indicate uncertainty on the part of the transcriber.

Participants: Alan Davies (father); Anne Davies (mother); three daughters: Sara (11 years), Megan (7 years), Hester (5 years).

1 *Anne:*   Meggie's had a very good sleep has she . . . she was fast asleep oh no she wasn't asleep

2 *Alan:*   come on Meggie do you want porridge

3 *Megan:* yes please

4 *Anne:*   it seemed to me you were asleep when (?) with Hester

5 *Megan:* yes

6 *Anne:*   but you weren't

7 *Megan:* I know I wasn't

8 *Anne:*   were you still reading then

9 *Sara:*   they were both wideawake when I was when I went up . . .

10 *Hester:* I was . . . up watching television at 10 o'clock . . . Mum

11 *Anne:*   Mm no you weren't

12 *Hester:* yes I was

13 *Anne:*   (now listen) you were very (*cough*) naughty to come down again . . . (?) (it means) you just get worn out

14 *Hester:* I didn't yawn
15 *Anne:* I said worn out
16 *Hester:* I didn't yawn out
17 *Anne:* I didn't say yawn out I said worn out
18 *Hester:* what's that mean
19 *Anne:* tired
20 *Hester:* I'm not tired didn't (*? ?*) that wasn't tired
21 *Anne:* who's going to give pussy his food . . .
22 *Sara:* mumsie mummy
23 *Anne:* Meggie would you (*?*) give him his kittie kat
24 *Megan:* what
25 *Anne:* would you give puss his kittie kat
26 *Hester:* pussie
27 *Megan:* certainly
28 *Anne:* oh well thank you very much
29 *Megan:* saucer (*??*)
30 *Anne:* just wondering if the tin's open . . .
31 *Megan:* (*?*) when you have to put masks on to smells . . . putting masks on to smells (*laughs*)
32 *Hester:* (*?*)
33 *Anne:* I think we haven't heard (*?*) from Ilfra for ages
34 *Alan:* come and sit down please
35 *Megan:* (*?*)
36 *Anne:* I think Ilfra's given us up . . . (funny) we haven't heard from Ilfra for such ages isn't it
37 *Hester:* (but) she gave us these
38 *Anne:* mm . . .
39 *Hester:* these make it looser
40 *Anne:* it feels a knot . . . oh well
41 *Hester:* I can put it back

An examination of Text 2 shows three different but equally important character-istics of spoken language. The first is the ellipsis, due largely no doubt to the shared understanding of the family members: who is Ilfra? (line 33); what does line 31 mean? – this line was so elliptical that even Megan could not restore the meaning after hearing a play-back shortly after the recording.

The second is the many hesitation features: zero pauses shown by dots in transcript; listener code markers, for example *yes, what, oh, mm*, listener code markers, for example *but, yes, well, mm*; reversals, for example *when I was when I went up.*

The third is the distribution of function: Alan's utterances (as father?) are predominantly directive, Anne's (as mother?) predominantly phatic, and the children's largely relatable to the other functions. Hester, the youngest child, seemed to have a mainly poetic function (the exchange in lines 13–20 shows how language learning can take place through word play). From a speech event point of view the whole breakfast could be classified as one speech event and thereby labelled as predominantly phatic, but that is a reductionist direction. The point surely is that the main language function of family meals is to rehearse solidarity among members by giving repeated opportunities for being together. Talk takes place but is typically random, moving arbitrarily from topic to topic; there is very little discussion about food (here only the one reference to porridge).

Abercrombie's term *spoken prose*, by which he refers to the common view of conversation, is quite unlike our Text 2 since Text 2 illustrates only a first remove from a phonetic transcription of natural speech. 'Strictly speaking, phonetic transcription records not an utterance but an analysis of an utterance' (Abercrombie 1963). Our Text 2 is already further idealized from the transcription stage, although it is still not yet at what Abercrombie calls spoken prose, at which stage hesitation features are removed,with subsequent changes made and punctuation added. Our Text 2 is somewhere between the transcription stage and the spoken prose stage. But it is spoken prose that is somehow thought to be what conversation is really like.

Text 3 (Spoken) is part of a recording made after a school visit to the Royal Highland Show in Edinburgh at which the horse-shoeing competition was the focus of attention. Text 3 (Written) is part of a written account by one of the schoolboys after the visit (Davies 1973).

Text 3 (Spoken)

Boy:	yeh, kept hammering it into shape until there's hardly – and he kept on till equal thickness
Teacher:	mm mm
Boy:	and length, and then bored eh holes seven holes in the shoe for seven nails
Teacher:	seven
Boy:	yeh
Teacher:	that's interesting . . . why seven
Boys:	it's three it's three on each side and
Boy:	one in the middle
Teacher:	one in the back . . . they have it . . . which way does the shoe face

Text 3 (Written)

First of all they made the shoes then hammered them into the horse's hoof. Before they put it on they had to file the horse's feet and make it clean. Then they made holes into the shoe to put the nails in. First he measured the metal and cut it to the right size. Then he placed the metal into a furnace.

I will make five points by way of comparison between these two versions (although we must bear in mind that these two texts were not the product of the same person):

1 The existential nature of speech: this is a point we have already made and it refers to the fact that what we have written down as Text 3 (Speech) is our interpretation of what was said whereas Text 3 (Written) actually exists as we have presented it.

2 The quantity of speech: speech is more discursive than writing, there is much more of it.

3 Speech is directly interactional, writing is not: we see this in Text 3 (Speech) in the interchanges between the teacher and the boy.

4 Speech is unplanned, writing is planned. There is a common occurrence in speech, a sort of wild-goose chase, moving from topic to topic in ways which are completely irrelevant to the discussion. This is less obvious in Text 3 much more in Text 2 as we have seen.

5 Speech is part of normal behaviour, writing is deliberate. And because the writer is not there to back up and explain there is an overwhelming tendency in writing to try to be clear and avoid ambiguity.

Writing has none of the immediacy of the spoken language (with the possible exception of an urgent note/letter/telex, etc): it is generally deliberate. As such it has none of the excuses of immediacy and spontaneity that we can use to explain the incoherence of speech. We expect writing therefore to be made up of grammatical 'sentences'. (Notice that these are text sentences *not* system sentences.)

Correctness

Community attitudes to the spoken language are less rigid than to the written (Warburg 1961). Correctness looms smaller but it still looms. We are still unsure about our acceptance of some fragments of English, partly because they may be thought characteristic of a disadvantaged part of the speech community, partly because doublets exist and we are unsure which one is more correct. The habit of language uncertainty is widespread. People seem to feel that their language can be located on a class scale relative to others above and below. It is more useful to regard such usages as more or less *appropriate* rather than correct or incorrect.

Correctness worries us at each of the language levels: how do you pronounce *controversy* or *Doncaster* or *often* (phonological – and normally resolved by purely social criteria); how do we choose between *shall* and *will*, between *who (did you ask . . .)* and *whom (did you ask . . .)* and between *you and me/I* (grammatical); what do we do with words like *get* and how do we distinguish between *disinterested/ uninterested* and *imply/infer* (lexical); and how do we keep finding new expressions for those difficult contexts, sex, religion and defecation (contextual). In all these cases there are choices; this is probably inherent in the idea of correctness; you can't be correct unless you've made a choice of some kind.

The main battleground for correctness is likely to be grammar since we are all operating within the one major system of Standard English. The arguments therefore are often among speakers of Standard English about little corners of their shared territory. They are arguments about such uncertainties as interrogative *who*, about the concord of *is*, about the position of *only*, *merely*, *hardly*, *just*, about the double participle *showed* and *shown* and so on; about *like* and *as*, about *it's me* and *it's I*, about *owing to* and *due to*, about *to John and I/me*.

First, the region of uncertainty is small. There can't be more than about forty items which are in dispute. Second, it is more a problem for the written language where we are concerned with a much more restricted conservative set of conventions. The choices are social rather than linguistic and it is as well for everyone to be clear on this. This sort of correctness is quite different from dialectal correctness, from the relation between Standard English and other dialects of English. But again it is a matter of convention. Dialects are all systematic, and therefore correctness is not at issue for them; they are all correct in their own terms. We may however choose to regard the errors that *second* language learners of English make as incorrect. However, there too one theory of second language acquisition argues that what such learning exemplifies is a systematic *interlanguage* (Ellis 1985). If that is so, it is not very helpful to make use of the concept of error and therefore of correctness and incorrectness.

Norms, the standard language and the home language

The new National Curriculum for England and Wales (the two Cox Reports: DES 1988b; 1989) are to be welcomed for the importance they give to the spoken language. Helpfully they also recognize the importance of the written language and that the base for that is Standard English.

The importance of literacy in giving greater access to ideas and information is widely accepted but there is a long-running dispute as to how crucial a role literacy has in individual cognitive development (Street 1984; Goody 1987). One famous study (Scribner and Cole 1981) concludes that it is not literacy but schooling that is decisive in individual development. The more general consensus seems to be that while the function of argument and explicit account fulfilled by writing can be carried by the spoken language (Finnegan 1988) they generally aren't. That is to say that while organized science flourishes in literate societies, scientific thinking is not out of the question for orate, non-literate societies. Literacy is therefore best seen as a habitual performance, as an important social rather than psychological activity. It matters in the way that learning another language or computing matter, because they too give greater access to information, rather than being a necessary stage in individual mental development.

There is a need to avoid humbug about the value of the standard language. The standard language, it will be remembered, we have associated particularly with the written language. It is more useful perhaps to see it as the dialect of the educated: their written and spoken codes represent the standard language therefore in the different ways we have described.

For the last part of this chapter, I want to present the opposing views as I see

108 SPOKEN ENGLISH ILLUMINATED

them in the language/code debate as they have been dramatically presented in publications during the 1980s. What I shall suggest is that the apparent permissiveness of the linguistic views has led to a stern rebuttal from an educational standpoint, an antithesis which bizarrely seems to say many of the right things but for the wrong reason. The protagonists I shall present are Peter Trudgill and John Honey (a fuller discussion is in Davies 1984).

Trudgill (1975) makes a strong case for the use of non-standard dialects in education. In a later publication he writes

> In educational circles this contrast between Standard English and the non-standard dialects is currently the focus of some considerable debate. To what extent, the question has been asked, are we justified in continuing to encourage and reward the use of Standard English in British schools?
>
> (Trudgill 1983: 193)

It appears that he is referring to *spoken* English since he does say: 'It is certainly true that all reading materials are written in Standard English and that many children learning to read have also to cope with a new and different dialect' (Trudgill 1983: 194–5). But even here he is ambivalent, suggesting that Standard written English does not need to be taught since the differences (from what? other varieties?) are 'not sufficient to cause great difficulties and most children appear to become skilled at translating as they go along, at a very early stage' (1983: 195). Trudgill points out quite correctly that 'grammatical forms which are most typical of working-class dialects have low status, because of their association with groups who have low prestige in our society' (1983: 205) and comments 'If children suffer because of attitudes to non-standard dialects it is the attitudes that should be changed and not the dialects' (1983: 206). Trudgill also suggests that society is becoming more relaxed about accents, as witness a wider range of accents among radio and television presenters, announcers and so on, and sees this as a sign that our attitudes have relaxed, the implications being that if attitudes to accent can change so can attitudes to dialect.

But I query whether society's attitudes to accent have seriously changed. Macaulay's account of self-stigmatizing Glaswegian children (Macaulay and Trevelyan 1975) still rings true. We now accept a wider range of accents on television and radio because we now have a much wider variety of programmes, and on the entertainment slots regional (not strong regional) and class (again not very marked) accents are, as it were, licensed. But on the 'serious' news and comment slots the presenters (including the ethnic talking heads) use modified RP or prestige regional, Scots or Irish.

Trudgill proposes slightly different treatments for various minority groups. For working-class children, he says that society's attitudes must change. For West Indian or Caribbean children, he suggests (1983: 194) that what would be helpful is a recognition, especially by teachers, that some West Indian children in British schools may be faced with what is perhaps best described as a semi-foreign language problem; that is while they have a problem, it is a problem not with Standard English but with British/English as a whole.

This seems an odd position to take up since most 'Caribbean' children now in the schools here were born in the UK. And for Scottish children Trudgill says that

> while social dialect continua ranging from local dialect to Standard English are found in much of England, in lowland Scotland . . . there is discontinuity because of the greater linguistic differences involved. . . . Many Scottish children are well aware that they have one dialect for school and another for other situations.
>
> (Trudgill 1983: 190–1)

Trudgill concludes that while 'translation' is possible from standard to non-standard dialect and children learn early how to do it, the 'problem' must be a question of social attitudes. The only reason he claims for teaching Standard English is that it is socially advantageous, that is not linguistically or cognitively so.

To dismiss linguistic advantage in this way, as Trudgill does, implies either that children do not need access to the range of written material, most of which is in Standard English, or that they will acquire Standard English anyway – in which case what is the fuss about? It isn't linguistic, says Trudgill, it's social attitudes; it's a matter of giving prestige to the children's home speech and not denigrating it explicitly or implicitly by denying it a school role. He is presumably talking here, as we have noted although it is not clear, only about spoken English. In the case of writing there are two major problems. First, there are no accepted conventions in most cases of how to write down dialect forms; second, in the absence of sophisticated linguistic training, trying to distinguish between correct and incorrect dialect forms would be an impossible burden on teachers. How would one write, for example, '*mi asks di man fi put mi moni iina him pakit*' (I asked the man to put the money in my pocket (Sutcliffe 1982))?

Honey (1983) has put himself forward as Trudgill's antagonist. Honey considers that standards have declined, civilization is collapsing and the barbarians are at the gate. 'It is a serious matter that our educational system . . . continues to turn out . . . an annual crop of total illiterates' (1983: 3). The responsibility lies, he claims, not with the schools but with 'a group of specialists in linguistics propagating the notion that for schools to foster one variety of English is contrary to the findings of the science of linguistics' (1983: 3). 'What we are dealing with is the theory of functional optimism', which seems to be a way of representing the linguistic view of the potential equality of all languages. Honey does not help his case when he complains that 'we have not been given any evidence that all languages or dialects have a grammatical structure of equal complexity' (1983: 17). But what is equal complexity? How would one show that say English and French have equal complexity?

But Honey's 'cause' is worthy of more serious attention:

For schools to foster non-standard varieties of English is to place their pupils in a trap. To persuade such speakers that their particular non-standard variety of English is in no way inferior, no less efficient for purposes of communication, but simply different, is to play a cruel trick. All the evidence we have suggests that listeners filter the message they receive from utterances of other speakers in accordance with perceptions of those speakers which are heavily influenced by the standard or non-standard nature of the language of the utterance in question.

(Honey 1983: 21-2)

It is difficult, says Honey, to change attitudes to dialects. Furthermore, the local dialect is not necessarily romantic; it can be given a sentimental value which puts limits in advance on children's 'ability to express themselves outside their immediate subculture, and to slam the door on any real opportunity for social mobility' (1983: 24-5). And he blames linguists for their support of linguistic diversity.

The apparent positions which are taken up stereotypically: 'Standard English does not need to be taught even for writing' (Trudgill) and 'Standard English only should be recognized in the schools' (Honey) can surely be reconciled. Between an individual idiolect and the social standard language there are certain non-standard dialects. To promote these as a school policy is divisive but they must be accepted and welcomed as part of the children's being and identity. To attempt to eradicate spoken dialect forms from individual speech (as against a bidialectal policy of adding standard forms) will not work. The goal in the schools must be decided educationally not linguistically; it must surely be to promote production and understanding of Standard written English and understanding of Standard spoken English; and it must tolerate production, where appropriate, of non-standard dialect English in the spoken form.

The argument is more about identity than about language. If children's home language is ignored or scorned they may suffer alienation. If the home dialect/language is given official status (as the medium of spoken interaction) there is the danger of functional divergence and eventual diglossia for those bidialectal groups for whom the written language may thus become fossilized, static, not amenable to change, and therefore something with which the children themselves cannot identify.

A discussion by R. Coates some years ago (1982) recognizes helpfully that standardization is an attempt to solve and not to create a problem. He makes the excellent point that standardization is inevitable and that it symbolizes integrative aspiration towards the social group whose norm is represented by distributions of standard pronunciation features:

for those involved in education, standardization can be seen as a litmus paper for a pupil's self-identification with the demands of school and a willingness to meet them practically even at the cost of distancing him or herself from (the language of the) peer group.

(R. Coates 1982: 41)

The tension between change and stability is seen once again in the relation between dialect and standard; the mark of a healthy education is that it promotes change without sacrificing stability. The Standard and the dialect are not incompatible – both are needed. In the same way the written language and the spoken language are both necessary in the educational process. What matters is that they should both be valued for what it is they can do uniquely, *speech* particularly for interaction and inclusion; *writing* particularly for coherence of argument; and also for what they each have to offer the other. Here the bridging role of literature is obvious.

Both speech and writing can gain from an orderly analytic exposure to a range of registers, styles and genres; both surely gain from an exposure of quantity, giving as much practice in varieties of speaking and writing. And both can also gain from what education can do so much better than the home – which is why education should not attempt to simulate home but do what it uniquely can do – and that is to create the conditions for reflection on the written and the spoken language, perhaps most of all, since we are accustomed to it for the written language, for reflection on the spoken language. This is the educated interest in giving due consideration not only to what one is talking about – that is often done – but also to how one is talking. And of course for that to be at all effective, and to enlist the students' interest in the analysis as something worth doing, teachers need to learn some of the skills of conversation analysis and discourse analysis. Enjoyment and amazement and excitement in the creativity of language use all have their place in learning, but the flip side of learning requires analysis. It is through analysis *and* enjoyment that the spoken language – and therefore, as we have argued, the language – can develop *for* the learner and *through* the learner.

PART FOUR

The assessment of oracy

Very little is known about the marking of spoken English, but it seems likely that the same conditions apply, and that the best judgements will be by impression. This does not however exempt the markers from a previous training in the recognition of the qualities which should go to make up their judgements.

The candidate's own teacher could carry out the test and mark it; another teacher from the same school could do it; they could do it jointly, marking separately and then comparing results. If part of the final oral mark is to be made up from the candidate's work over a period, then clearly his teacher will have to have a good deal of the responsibility for the mark. In Tasmanian schools, 50% of the mark is made up by this means, an official record sheet is kept which advises, 'Assessments may be made incidentally on group discussion, plays, choral speaking, talks, prose reading, general participation, and any other oral work taken during the year.'

(Wilkinson 1965: 82 and 79–80)

12 Truth to tell: criteria for judgement

ANDREW WILKINSON and
DEBORAH BERRILL

The present position

In assessing oracy two important questions are 'Where?' and 'How?' The first
question – Where? – is easily answered; not in decontextualized situations, but
where it is part and parcel of the pupil's ongoing learning in the classroom, school
or community. In *Spoken English* we wrote

> Where children are given responsibility they are placed in situations where it
> becomes important for them to communicate – to discuss, to negotiate, to converse –
> with their fellows, with the staff, with other adults. And of necessity they are likely to
> develop oral skills. This basically is how oracy grows; it is to be taught by the creation
> of the many and varied circumstances to which both speech and listening are the
> natural responses.
>
> (Wilkinson 1965: 59)

It follows that assessment should essentially take place in such circumstances –
no one task, no one occasion, can be representative. This is beginning to be
recognized. Thus *English for Ages 5 to 16* (the second Cox Report: DES 1989)
notes as the first important criterion for national assessment:

> the assessment of speaking and listening should, where possible, be informal,
> continuous and incidental, applied to tasks carried out for curricular purposes.
>
> (DES 1989: 15.43)

Commonly teachers will have a card with headings of various oral activities –
group discussion, story-telling, responded to extended long turns, role-play, and
so on – and record individual performances. Not every pupil is assessed on every
occasion, and achievement rather than average performance is looked for, so that
over a period a profile of the best the individual has offered is built up. Whether
this is expressed in the form of statements, a single grade or a number of grades is
a political not an educational decision.

The second question – How? (i.e. by what criteria?) – is less easily answered.
Work in certain specific areas – Sinclair and Coulthard on the language of

teachers and pupils (1975), and Barnes and Todd (1977) on learning in small groups – puts all subsequent students in their debt. But this is fundamental research. For our present purposes we need to glance at criteria in use in practical assessments currently operating.

In this connection the important work of the Assessment of Performance Unit (Gorman *et al.* 1984; Brooks 1987) in their national 'light-sampling' in the UK should be noted. Their analytical marking has the general categories of sequential structure, lexico-grammatical features (lexical selection and syntax), and performance features (hesitancy/fluency, tempo/pacing, verbal assertiveness). The purpose of the analytic marking was to provide insights into which specific features of talk contributed to the variation in the overall impression (holistic) marking, which had initially been carried out for 'communicative effectiveness' and 'orientation to listener'. The criteria are very useful, but less suited to reciprocal than to extended speech, and this is perhaps explained by the brief of the research, which tended to prompt long turns in its tasks. The researchers attempted to supply contexts but these could obviously not be those of day-to-day classroom learning. (For contrasting assessments of this work see papers by Gorman *et al.*, Rosen, and MacLure in Mercer 1988.)

A study by Brown *et al.* (1984) uses strictly constrained, decontextualized tasks, all 'information-related', concerned with the construction of long turns. It draws up criteria related to them, basically rewarding the information communicated, but these criteria are task-specific and thus not of general application. The term 'information-related tasks' is very limiting, especially when there are hints that it probably means 'cognitive tasks' in the minds of the researchers. This is an important line, insufficiently followed up.

A good deal has been done by examining boards in UK on the assessment of oracy and in the General Certificate of Secondary Education (GCSE), a common examination for all at 16, it is a compulsory element. There is pressure for assessment in North America and Australasia, and the policy of the UK government is for compulsory testing of all school-children at ages 7, 10, 13 and 16, with oracy as one of the 'Profile Components'. It is clear that much more research needs to be carried out in the field, such as that in progress by Pringle and Fox in connection with the Oral Language Portfolio for the Oral Assessment Instrument Pool in Ontario (Pringle and Fox 1987; Fox and Pringle 1988).

Briefly the present situation is that, despite all the excellent work carried out over the past twenty-five years, there is as yet no satisfactory philosophical basis for the assessment of oracy, no comprehensive workable model, no unifying principle. Painstaking lists of criteria have been drawn up. Yet often they have not distinguished between the largely different activities involved in reciprocal and extended utterance. Commonly they have not sorted trivial from significant features. Sometimes they have been so complicated as to be quite unusable.

What follows is an attempt to construct a model free from the above defects and justifiable on rational principles.

Frames of language

In every day life we make judgements about people's oral abilities. We say they 'talk sense' or 'talk nonsense', 'have some good ideas', 'haven't got an idea in their heads'. We may say they are 'fluent' or 'garrulous', are 'a good listener' or 'just don't listen to a word'. We say they 'don't know when to stop', 'can't organize their thoughts', 'don't stick to the point', are 'good with words', can 'never find the right word'. The first group of comments refers to the content of what people say, the second group to their presentation and ability to relate to others, and the third to the choice of words and forms they use. Thus in popular parlance we find some basis for oral assessment.

If we translate these ideas into linguistic terms, not just for the secret pleasure of using jargon, but because these terms carry an additional wealth of meaning, we find that we have stumbled on a well-established linguistic classification. Halliday (1970: 143) would classify the first as the Ideational aspect of language: 'Language serves for the expression of "content": that is, of the speaker's experience of the real world, including the inner world of his own consciousness'. The second – how things are said – would be called the Interpersonal aspect: 'language serves to establish and maintain social relations for the expression of social roles . . . and also for getting things done by means of interaction between one person and another'. The third – the words and forms chosen – is the Textual; the speaker or writer 'constructs "texts" or connected passages of discourse that [are] situationally relevant'.

Ideational aspect

'Content' is basically information of some kind: 'It is cold'. But information itself is only a start; more important is what we do with it. First, what do we think about it? 'It is cold – and therefore I won't bathe' is where we use it to draw a conclusion. Second, what do we feel about it? 'Curse the cold, I hate it when it's cold' – where we use it as an object of emotion. We think and feel about our experience, and in this way construct our world and relate to it. Not all information is of the same validity of course. It may be partial, limited, prejudiced, untrue, and this would affect our perceptions and behaviour. If it were not cold we could have bathed after all.

Thus the ideational aspect of talk is the information it contains and the thinking and feeling it represents. Thinking and feeling are not completely separate: we move between the two and the one is often tinged with the other. 'It is cold' can be both a thought and an expression of feeling. Even so we can properly talk about the 'quality of thinking' and the 'quality of feeling' as a matter of convenience.

The quality of thinking

It is possible to speak with some confidence of different levels of thinking, or 'cognition'. Piaget gave the classic statement of the growth of cognition (see e.g.

Piaget and Inhelder 1969), and although it has been shown that his experiments underestimated the performance of young children (Donaldson 1978), his general structure proves useful. Work by Moffett (1968), Peel (1971), Britton *et al.* (1973) and Wilkinson *et al.* (1980) have applied such views to written language. So far however there has not been an attempt to examine systematically cognition in spoken language.

This is what we wish to do, drawing on and adapting the 'cognitive model' used for writing in the Crediton Project (Wilkinson *et al.* 1980; Wilkinson 1986a). We wrote: 'The basis of this model is a movement from an undifferentiated world to a world organised by mind, from a world of instances to a world related by generalities and abstractions' (Wilkinson *et al.* 1980: 2).

The lowest level of cognition is 'describing' (labelling, recording, reporting). Then comes 'interpreting' (explaining, inferring, deducing). Next is 'generalizing' (summarizing, reflecting, classifying). The highest level is 'speculating' (hypothesizing, projecting, theorizing). It is important to emphasize that these items can be meaningful as a hierarchy only in relation to the degree of abstraction, complexity and quality of information they use.

The quality of feeling

In considering feeling it is less easy than with cognition to point to a generally agreed description of development. In the Crediton Project we took what seemed to be a practical consensus about what constitutes emotional maturity – an ability to express our own emotions and to have insight into them; an empathy with others; a non-exploitative view of the human-created and natural world; and a positive stance towards the stresses and shocks of life – 'coping', in popular parlance. At such goals we never arrive – we are always arriving. We summed this up as follows:

> [Affective development] is seen as being in four movements – one towards a greater awareness of self, a second towards a greater awareness of neighbour as self, a third towards a greater awareness of the non-human environment, and a fourth towards a stance towards the human condition.
>
> (Wilkinson 1986a: 15)

A simplified lay-out, not in ascending order, would be:

> Self becoming aware – motives, context, image of self;
> Self becoming aware of neighbour as self, others;
> Self becoming aware of, respecting, physical, social environment;
> Self – coming to terms with the human condition, 'reality'.
>
> (Wilkinson 1986a: 15)

Interpersonal aspect

The question we need to ask about the use of interpersonal language is: how do speakers and listeners relate to one another? How far do they understand and respond to one another? In group discussion evidence of this will be given in the way in which speakers pick up one another's points and the use they make of them. Sensitivity might be displayed both to the meaning offered and to the person offering it, as when a hesitant remark by a nervous speaker is acknowledged and supported by a more confident one. And there are a variety of 'rules' (about 'turn-taking' for instance) and 'roles' to carry on the conversation. In the various forms of extended utterance, however, quite a different situation applies. Usually there is only one rule – that the speaker is not interrupted. With longer turns, such as talks, telling stories, etc., there is a range of 'presentational' skills not really required in discussion – clarity and quality of voice, intonation, timing, etc. Speakers are certainly influenced by the listeners in the sense that they should be able to monitor continuously their sub-verbal (laughter, murmurs) and non-verbal responses.

Textual aspect

The 'text' is the words uttered. They do not have to be written down to constitute a text (though for the purposes of analysis a transcription is very useful). The Crediton Project (Wilkinson *et al.* 1980; Wilkinson 1986a) listed six features of style useful in describing a text. In that research it was a written text, but the features are also present in oral text. We can look at its organization, cohesion, syntax, lexis, sense of listeners, and appropriateness.

In extended (long turn) utterance the *organization* of the whole will be under the control of the speaker, as will its cohesion (the linking of its separate items, e.g. sentences together). One common form of organization is chronological – to begin at the beginning and go on till the end. A story does this but differs from a chronology in being perhaps more selective and having linkages other than temporal between the parts. Another structure is argumentative – points for, points against presented, followed by a conclusion.

But in reciprocal utterance, as in discussion, no single person is in control, and a particular remark may move the participants in a completely different direction. This often happens in conversation where someone says 'By the way . . .' and starts a new hare. Or when there is a silence and someone else fills it by a new initiative ('Tell me, Goneril, do you know a good pharmacist?'). How far talk keeps on a particular track depends on such factors as its purpose and the participants. There are various forms of talk and thus various forms of organization. *Cohesion* will exist not in the whole piece but only in the linking of one turn to another.

The *syntax* of sentences will commonly vary as between reciprocal and extended utterances. One might expect it to be more fragmented or incomplete in the former, more complete, more complex in the latter. But much depends on the participants and the occasion. The *lexis* – vocabulary – in its literal, idiomatic and metaphorical uses is central to the communication. In certain types of extended utterance, such as telling of a traditional story, one might expect literary metaphorical language. In short turn utterances, such as chat, on the other hand, there is likely to be colloquial idiom and banal phraseology.

A *sense of the listener* might be expected to occur more readily in discussion than in extended utterance. In the former, speakers are constantly subjected to feedback from the other members of the group, while in the latter they have to pluck it from the eyebrows of their audience. A similar factor affects the *appropriateness* of the language used – it is often far easier to relate to a small group than to a large, possibly unknown, audience. (In the Model of Assessment set out on p. 123 a sense of 'listener' is treated under the Interpersonal rather than the Textual heading.)

Telling the truth

We have discussed (pp. 115–16) the lack of a theoretical base, a unifying principle, for the assessment of oracy. That one exists, however, becomes clear if we ask ourselves what is the purpose of the spoken (indeed of all) language. Obviously to communicate – but to communicate what? The answer is, simply, the truth.

People's contributions to a conversation ought to be truthful. We should not say anything which we believe to be false, or for which we have no adequate evidence. This observation by Grice (1975) has important implications beyond conversation. (This matter has been broached in Chapter 8.) In conversation itself we can of course lie, but at the expense of our credibility. Again, in day-to-day life if you ask the way and are sent in the opposite direction, or if you miss a train because Train Enquiries deliberately misinforms you, then the whole social system begins to suffer.

However, things are very different in literature and the arts. Here the biggest lies are the most popular. Goldilocks and the three bears – what nonsense! Macbeth and the three witches – what utter falsehood! And yet we not only enjoy these fictions ourselves but also encourage our innocent children to do so. In fact in literature we require 'imaginative truth'. On the one hand this means that, when we are reading a story or watching a play, we believe in what is happening. However fantastic it may be, for the time being we accept it in order to enjoy it. As Coleridge puts it we undergo 'a willing suspension of disbelief'. On the other hand it means that the story or play has some significance for us. King Lear may never have existed but Shakespeare's play tells us something about the problems and pathos of old age and is in that sense 'true'.

Thus truthfulness – either literal or imaginative – is a characteristic, not just of conversation, but of all forms of language. Let us consider how it may be presented in conversation. A group of 5-year-olds in a first school are talking to a visitor sitting at their table with them.

Kelly: I'm making an Easter basket.
Gemma: I'm painting mine green and pink.
William: James has spoilt his. He's cut this off (*shows tab cut off*)
James: (*ruefully*) Yes, I have. I'm poor with scissors.

There are four statements made. The evidence for the first two is immediately visual: James gives small demonstration for the third. The fourth is in the nature of himself by James, who explains why it has happened. The need to support our assertions is a common one because we need to feel justified, to be believed.

Again, let us take four 7-year-olds:

Steven: Anybody here likes fishing?
Jason: Pardon?
Eve: I like fishing.
Jason: I've never been fishing in my life.
Edward: I like it.
Jason: And I've got a fishing rod.
Steven: Well I've been fishing in Blicking Lake before the . . .

(Shea 1988: 42)

All make statements. Eve's and Edward's are offered as a matter of their preferences. Steven supports his by the evidence of a visit, Jason by the irony of his never having fished though he has a fishing rod (an implied evaluation – what do you think of that!).

With this group of 13-year-olds discussing family history, validations for the action of Alan's grandfather in joining the army are the main theme:

Alan: My grandad joined the army. He didn't have to. He was in a reserved occupation.
Sue: What's that?
Alan: When you were in some jobs you didn't have to join up.
Sue: So why did he?
Alan: Well his friends had.
Pat: So he'd have felt left out.
Greg: Might have said he was soft.
Alan: Yes, but he wanted to anyway.
Sue: Why?
Alan: Said it was the right thing to do.

Sue's role here is to probe terms and motives, Alan's to supply explanations, in which he is supported empathetically by Pat and Greg.

In a confrontational argument validation is particularly important. Here are two 15-year-olds on entitlement to a wage award. A makes a statement which he then supports by one argument in his own favour and a second against his opponent.

A: I think the pay rise should be mine because I've got to travel to work and it's quite a bit of a way and I've got to pay for petrol and 'cos you live on a ship you don't have to travel very far.
      (*B replies in terms of the greater responsibility he carries.*)
B: Yes but I have – I end up doing other people's jobs as well especially the apprentices when they're coming in I've got to do something for them to show them how to do it.

(APU 1984: 223)

Dialogue consists mainly of statements and questions. One of the chief functions of questions is to establish the truth of statements, and the quality of their validation. These 8-year-olds are engaged in an island project:

Jenny: So they're going to escape on a boat.
Christopher: How do you know?
Jenny: It says so on the paper.
Shauna: You've got to make it up.
Christopher: They can't make a boat . . .
Shauna: Yes they can.
Christopher: Because they haven't got a boat – I mean a hammer and nails.
Guido: You said they haven't got a boat, that's silly.

Jenny's validation for her statement is the hand-out issued. Shauna offers an alternative. Christopher then comes in with reasons at the practical level. An interesting feature of this interchange is the 'evaluation' – Christopher's of his own statement, correcting what he has said, and Guido's (somewhat gratuitous) drawing attention to it.

Information, validation, evaluation

We have thus examined briefly three elements in spoken language – the *information* it offers, the *validation* this receives, and the *evaluation* provided. And the quality of these is important.

Information can be true or false, original or conventional, fair or prejudiced, partial or complete, well known or little known, and so on. Overall in popular parlance we normally like speakers to be 'well informed' when they are talking, to cause us to think – that's interesting, new, original, accurate, personal, relevant. We do not think without information. One of the reasons that young children do not think as well as older children is that they know less. This information does not need to be factual; it could be speculative: 'Let us suppose', said Galileo, 'that the earth moves round the sun.' It could be imaginative: 'The owl and the pussy cat went to sea . . .'

Validation can be entirely in terms of the speaker. If someone says, 'I feel tired', this is a complete validation. We cannot answer, 'You think you feel tired, but you aren't really.' Again, there is expert validation. We accept doctors' opinions on medical matters because they have the training we believe qualifies them to speak. A doctor's advice on your carburettor may be another matter. On the other hand doctors are more and more explaining to patients. And in fact explanations are the kinds of validations we customarily give in our everyday conversations with people. Explanations have a varying quality for valuation. A young child instructed not to run may ask why. His mother could reply, 'Because you mustn't', 'Because I say so', 'Because mummy wouldn't like it', 'Because you might fall', 'Because the paving is uneven and you might trip'. These explanations move from the completely circular to that in terms of cause-and-effect. More complex explanations would be possible, such as 'As the consequence of a pernicious council policy designed to expose its opponents as soft-centred liberals, money has been spent on the police at the expense of civil amenities, with the result that . . .' And so on. It is doubtful whether the mother would feel it suitable to go into such detail, but there are situations where it would be appropriate.

Evaluation can be of the individuals by themselves ('I'm poor with scissors') of their own language and ideas ('What I mean to say is') or of the offerings of others ('You said they haven't got a boat – that's silly'). It can be of the general matter discussed; it can take the form of incidental summaries or final summings up. Basically what it shows is the play of mind over the text, and ability to stand at once inside and outside it.

Information, *validation* and *evaluation* – we have discussed these in various forms of reciprocal talk. They apply even more obviously to various forms of

The assessment of oracy: a model

Ideational (what is said)	Interpersonal (how it is said)	Textual (the form chosen)
Cognition describing interpreting generalizing speculating	*Roles* dominant co-operative supportive acquiescent passive disruptive	*Telling: long turns* story exposition report a talk etc.
Affect self-awareness awareness of others respect for environment stance towards the human condition	*Rules* based on consensus based on power	*Talking: short turns* gossip, chat conversation discussion interviews committee meeting etc.
	Presentation face and body language paralinguistics visual demonstration	
Consider quality of Information Validation Evaluation	*Consider* the effects on the listener(s)	*Consider* style organization cohesion syntax lexis appropriateness

extended utterance. Let us consider imaginative story-telling as an example. Here is a story by Amanda, who had just celebrated her fourth birthday:

> *Amanda:* Once upon a time a little mouse lived. And he couldn't have a hole because he was so fat, and he didn't have time to spare because he was so happy. And I didn't know what to do, so I had an idea, 'I'm giving him a new home'. So I did. That was in my mummy and daddy's room – there was a little mousehole.
>
> *Adult:* Was there?
>
> *Amanda:* And there there [sic] really is.

Amanda has a real sense of story, beginning with the traditional opening, then presenting a problem – that of a home for an overweight mouse – and then finding a solution to it, neither of which is traditional. The validation takes several forms. One is explanation – he didn't have a home 'because he was so fat': he didn't have time to look for one 'because he was so happy' (enjoying himself). Another is the exact detail – the little girl quotes her own thoughts, 'I'm giving him a new home' – and she specifies the mousehole – 'in my mummy and daddy's room'. A very interesting feature of this piece is Amanda's evaluation – 'there really is', i.e. this is a real mousehole I am talking about, not one made up.

In Amanda's story we have an interesting combination of the two forms of truth that we mentioned earlier, which we called for convenience literal and imaginative. In subsequent chapters we shall develop this idea of truth, its validation and evaluation, as an important part of our apprehension of oracy.

In the model we set out above we are concerned with spontaneous utterances, either in short turns (as in discussion, or conversation), or in 'long turns' (as in story telling, or giving an account). Basically (though there is of course overlap) these are the two ways the spoken language is used. Even non-spontaneous utterances (language written down to be spoken) fall into these two categories. Thus a play is in a sense a simulated conversation, a public speech, a premeditated long turn utterance. They are written forms which imitate some of the features of speech. (See Chapter 11 above.)

13 Long turn development: stories and directions

ANDREW WILKINSON

Language development

Language development obviously takes place, but does not take place obviously. It is not like climbing a ladder from one rung to another; it is more like the waves advancing on a beach, one wave making a gain, the next falling short of it. As the Cox Report says

> we recognise that language development is not linear but recursive, with pupils returning repeatedly to the same aspects of competence and reinforcing their skills on each occasion. In addition, what is difficult will vary for different individuals and according to circumstances: some topics will themselves vary in difficulty; some people will perceive the difficulty of the same task very differently; and circumstances may make an otherwise easy task seem hard.
>
> (DES 1989: 15.20)

Cox also recognizes that there is no exact correlation between age and development by proposing ten Levels of Attainment for speaking and listening. Thus at the first two levels, pupils should be able to

Level 1
  i Participate as speakers and listeners in group activities, including imaginative play.
 ii Listen attentively, and respond, to stories and poems.
iii Respond appropriately to simple instructions given by the teacher.

Level 2
  i Participate as speakers and listeners in a group engaged in a given task.
 ii Describe an event, real or imagined, to the teacher or another pupil.
iii Listen attentively to stories and poems and talk about them.
 iv Talk with the teacher, listen and ask and answer questions.
  v Respond appropriately to a range of more complex instructions given by a teacher, and give simple instructions.

Very few of these things could not have been carried out by the pre-school children described in Chapters 2–5 of this book, or by those in the research referred to there.

The authors of the report are aware of such limitations and beg that they are treading new ground (DES 1989: 15.44). As they say, exemplars will be needed. What is needed also is an assessment model with a set of criteria which will enable more exact discriminations to be made. This is what we have tried to construct in the previous chapter, and we shall now go on to apply some of criteria of our model to extended utterance (long turns) in this chapter, and to reciprocal utterance (short turns) in the next.

The development of story-telling, 5–11

There are various forms of 'telling', characterized by a 'long turn' – a story, anecdote, account of a process or a happening, a reminiscence, a talk, an exposition, a lecture. They may be uttered more or less spontaneously. On the other hand, if they are written down in order to be spoken aloud (perhaps read), they will tend to be written rather than spoken language. Many lectures, prepared statements and political speeches are of this kind.

Here we will consider one form of telling: the sort of story-telling which is not an act of the imagination but which is based on actual experience in the speaker's life. None of the examples following is a 'set-piece': all arise during normal activities in the classroom. The first four are from children sitting informally around the teacher in the home corner, and are part of an enjoyable swap-shop of experiences. The others are spoken to peer groups in which the speakers feel very comfortable.

Teresa

I went shopping with my Mum. And we went to Tesco's and we went to Debenhams, and my Mum bought me a coat in the sales.

Ideational: Information – a general statement, *validated* by the two illustrations (the supermarket and the department store), serving as a setting for the event.

Interactional: Teresa looks at the group unblinking with huge Spanish eyes, clasping one hand over a wrist. She speaks quite loudly as though this were an announcement for which she well knows the style of delivery. The second 'my Mum' is given great pride and emphasis. At the mention of the coat the eyes of two girls shine.

Textual: A chronological organization.

Tracey

My news is my friend and she's called Jenny. She's in Mrs Howes'. I don't play with her at dinner time, 'cos I'm a packed lunch, and she's a hot dinner. And that's all.

Ideational: The topic, 'friend', is denoted (*information*). This is then supported by identification of name and class (*validation*). The scene set, the main point comes – they don't play at dinner time – and a reason to validate it – we're in separate meal schedules – follows.

Interpersonal: Tracey is hugging herself, keeping her eyes down in a solemn face, and talking in rather a confiding tone. This alienation of friend from friend brought about by the system is a serious matter. She receives a nod of emphatic support from Michael, which he continues with as though mesmerized. Several are sympathetic, but William seems to be elsewhere. 'I like Big Macs,' he says. The teacher asks Michael if his head is loose.

Textual: Neither children nor teacher find anything strange in ''cos I'm a packed lunch, and she's a hot dinner'. Why should they? It is their normal usage.

Paul

> We started off, and gran gave us some nibbles and a drink first, then dinner, then pudding which was cheesecake and cheese, and there was raspberry, peach and strawberry. Then we all went to bed, and then in the morning we had breakfast. And then we went to a restaurant, and it was BRILLIANT.

Ideational: Bare items of *information* (though 'pudding' is exemplified). But the 'flavours' which seem to support either 'cheesecake' or 'cheese' in fact do neither. They are a separate item, unstated (yoghurts). Emotion is held close in until the last, but his sentence *evaluates*, at least for him, at least the restaurant, at most the whole visit.

Interpersonal: Paul, very fair, blue-eyed, erect, delivers in a clear almost military style, giving the items as a record, until he comes to his final sentence, 'and it was BRILLIANT'. The children like this recital of food, and Nigel draws in his breath.

Textual: A chronological 'bed-to-bed' (a bed-to-bed is a common form of young children's written composition in which the protagonist gets up, goes through the major events of the day, usually meals, and goes to bed again). Here the beds are absent but the food is very much present.

Kelly

> We went to Hunstanton in my Dad's car, and we saw this seal. It smelt horrid. My Mum said, 'Come away and let's tell somebody'. But two men came in a truck and we did not see what happened. We had ice-cream at the amusements, and I wasted my money. And my sister lost her bag. And that's all really.

Ideational: The first sentence orients us, and then there are three episodes – the seal, the amusements, the loss of the bag. A good deal of affect appears in the language about the seal, and in the tone of voice in the last episode. (Seals were dying in the North Sea from an infection related to distemper in dogs and were being washed up along the British coasts.) In each episode there is *evaluation* – concerning the seal in 'It smelt horrid' and in the shudder with which this is said. In 'the amusements' it lies in 'wasted my money' (on the pin machines), and in 'my sister lost her bag' in the tone in which this is said (meaning 'she would, wouldn't she?').

Interpersonal: Kelly has a Lebanese father, and long black plaits with red ribbons, but derives her local style from her Norfolk mother – there is a wryness in her tone when she speaks of 'wasting her money' and of her sister. There are signs of dramatic talent, in 'smelt horrid' – the children shudder with her, and she can change mood quickly to the last two episodes.

Textual: Chronological structure, stopping rather than finishing, in which she includes nothing irrelevant. 'Smells horrid' is effective for the meaning she gives it, and she uses 'wasted my money' with a certain irony. The meaning of 'my sister lost her bag' is in her paralinguistics and facial expression.

Struan

> Well, when we went to Scotland we went to Benderloch, and we went out to Trulee Bay – you see my granny lives there. And she lives very near the beach, so you see there was this speedboat on the beach, and this man who owned them let us go out on them. And we took a picnic lunch and it was FANTASTIC! We stayed in this little castle, OH BOY! We went down to see the dungeons, we went up and saw a few swords and armour. Oh it was FANTASTIC, that was OOH! And then we came back, and we went to another one, and it was terribly – it was exactly the same. But we went to the other side of the island, you see, because it was too far to walk (*laughs*). So we had to take the speedboat, and then we came back and then we went home.

Ideational: A general statement about the holiday followed by information about a particular day, explained where necessary ('you see my granny lives there', 'because it was too far to walk'). The great strength of this piece is in its affect – the enthusiasm Struan displays for the incident and the way he gets this across.

Interpersonal: Struan is a stocky fair Scottish boy, with a grin which keeps breaking into little laughs as he tells his story. Indeed he is known as a raconteur – phrases like 'you see' indicate his intimacy with his listeners. He talks quickly and with enthusiasm to which they respond with large shining eyes. When he uses the word 'FANTASTIC' first he perceives their excitement, and uses another 'hurrah' term 'OH BOY'. They glimmer delightedly in response. He knows he has got them and very successfully uses 'FANTASTIC' again. But not content with this he crowns his triumph by verbalizing the tingle running down their spines – 'OOH!' They are eating out of the palm of his hand.

Textual: Struan organizes chronologically. There are two episodes, the second starting 'And then we came back'. Here he begins by attempting to do the same thing, to enthuse the listeners again 'It was terribly . . . (exciting?)' but wisely abandons it – once is enough, so the second episode finishes tamely with their going home, though he does attempt to put some humour into it. He conveys emotion very effectively in three ways: one is by his attack and tone of voice; the second is by his use of emotionally toned words ('castle', 'dungeons', 'swords', 'armour' – these carry the message without additional description); and third is by use of words (and even non-words) whose referentional content is minimal but whose emotional content is high – 'fantastic', 'oh boy', 'ooh'.

Linda

> It was a few months ago, about half a year I think it was – we went, I think it was in Italy – and we went to a big tower, and it is one of the Seven Wonders of the World, and it was crooked – it went like that (*inclines hand*). And there were two hundred steps and we had to go all the way up, and I was the first one up, and I was almost blown off the side when the bells went. You had to put ear plugs in but we didn't have any, because we didn't know we were going to go.
>
> Then we had to go down again and then just across the road there was another place, when – I think it was round, with a long round roof on, and somebody came in and it made such an echo. It was very, very loud – he was talking softly and when he went in again it made a loud echo.
>
> And then after that we went down again, and we went down to the graveyard. I don't know if we were allowed in but we did go in. There were a few graves, and I wish I'd seen some bones but I didn't. I looked in every single grave that hadn't a grave top on, but I didn't find any.

Ideational: We start with the great advantage of unusual *information*. And further Linda, we might say, answers the questions of the curious (*validation*) – there is a background of rationality to this visit. Why was the effect of the bells so devastating? Because they had no earplugs. Why was that? They hadn't anticipated the trip (*evaluation* – and thus they were not to blame). Was there a reason why they shouldn't have entered the graveyard (*evaluation* – and thus a certain apprehension attached)? The affect is present, the excitement of heightened experience – 'almost blown off', 'it made such an echo', 'I wish I'd seen some bones but I didn't'. Linda is tentative ('think it was') and alternative possibilities ('I don't know if we were allowed in . . .')

Interpersonal: Linda's face, eyes, cheeks are ovals. She talks quickly and breathily and sounds as if it is all 'great fun'; her voice becomes more secret in the graveyard. She does not project or play the listeners like Struan (though she uses non-verbals) but they enjoy what she says because of its rarity and excitement.

Textual: Three separate incidents are connected not only temporally and locationally, but also by the enthusiasm of the teller. Each incident is developed sufficiently for its impact to be felt – this is not undifferentiated chronology. She knows how to rephrase for emphasis – notice how the last sentence, with its stress on 'every single grave' serves to polish the previous one.

Helen

> We had a very exciting holiday on Dartmoor this year. This was because we heard in the news and read in the newspapers that a prisoner had escaped from Dartmoor, and

he'd attacked a policeman. You see a policeman coming off duty on Dartmoor became suspicious that a van parked at the side of the road, and he went up to the man, the escaped prisoner who was beside the van, and he threw ammonia in his eyes. Now this could have been very dangerous because ammonia is a chemical, and it could have blinded the policeman. But fortunately the policeman managed to get into the nearest town and get help and he went to hospital. And the police set up road-blocks. Now road-blocks are not blocks of stone in the middle of the road or anything like that, but a policeman will stop you and show you a photograph of a man, the man, and ask you questions, if you've seen the man, or if you've heard anything, and that's all they are really.

And on our way on to Dartmoor once we were stopped by a man, a nice young policeman, and he described the escaped prisoner to us, and he was described as being gypsy-looking, small, heavy featured, and he had a red stripe down one of the sides of his jumper, had a shot gun. And the policeman was obviously very upset because he said to us, 'If you see him run him down – only don't say I said so'. And he must have been very upset because the policeman who was hurt must have been a mate of his and he was very worried. And as we got further on to Dartmoor there were more road-blocks, and this time, as well as showing us the photographs they checked our boot, only they couldn't have found much in our boot (*laughs*) because all there was was anoraks and picnic basket and deckchairs, and that was all really, so there was no room for a man in there.

It all turned out really well, fortunately, because the man wasn't blinded, and although you would think that through all those road-blocks there were on Dartmoor the man couldn't have escaped he did, but he was captured in Birmingham.

Ideational: The *information* offered is fresh, unusual. It's not the normal prisoner escape as on television but an incident the speaker has been involved in. Even more than Linda's it satisfies the questions of the curious – wherever an item needs support this is supplied (*validation*). There is the explanation of ammonia and its danger, the definition of road-blocks, negatively and positively (what one is and is not), the detailed description of the escapee, and the contents of the boot. (Probably much of this is new knowledge which Helen acquired from the events and which she takes pleasure in passing on.) *Evaluation* is taking place throughout, including the outcome ('It all turned out really well, fortunately'). In affective terms we see a sense of the humour of the incident as well as its serious side. And empathy is shown for the 'nice young policeman', hypothesizing about the reason for his particular distress and thus the nature of his language.

Interpersonal: Helen sits telling her story to her friends in the serenity of pre-adolescence, her blue eyes merry when she laughs about the thought of the prisoner hidden with the luggage. She talks quietly but clearly, sometimes pausing to plan her next statement: she does not want to leave anything out – and does not do so. The group participate with enjoyment – 'a nice young policeman' is put in for her girl-friends but the boys are also enjoying the adventure. (What would they have felt?) But she does not incite them to excitement. They are taken along by the intrinsic interest of the material, the details she chooses, and the way she leads to the denouement. Her skill is that she seems to let the story tell itself.

Textual: A summary statement begins as in so many stories, and then it is filled out in what follows in a narrative account which comes to a climax – the searching of the boot – and is followed by a denouement away from the immediate incident, in which two possibilities are scouted before one is chosen (you would think he couldn't escape – but he did). What sustains this extended language and makes it different from the recall of information in chronological form is the shaping action of an underlying story pattern.

Giving directions: 7–11

Four children give directions as to how to reach their homes from the school gate. The listeners are their peer groups, receptive and sympathetic.

Ideational

This task is essentially concerned with describing – with giving *information* – not with interpreting or hypothesizing. However this is not a simple thing. It requires an ability to use abstractions such as left and right, to select (a mass of detail is confusing) and to decentre – to be aware of what one's words mean to others.

Interactive

Decentring can also be seen as a function of the interactive aspect of language. If we are to be understood we are always to some extent attempting to enter the minds of others. We constantly make wrong guesses, and often have to repeat and reformulate accordingly.

Textual

The meaning conveyed is dependent on the words used, and their organization. In a situation like this the words need to be accurate, proper names need to be used, and significant landmarks denoted.

Karen

> Well, I'd come out of the school gate and cross with the Lollipop Lady. And I'd go down the very steep hill. I'd cross this road, the main road. Then there's a path. I'd walk along that path, and then there's another hill. There is a road, and I'd cross that road. When I get to the other side I'm the second house.

Karen is following the route home in her mind's eye, and is unable to perceive it from another's viewpoint. 'This road', 'a path', 'another hill' are meaningless to a third party. She does not select significant detail, indicate orientation, or give the names of roads, etc.

Gavin

> Well you come out of the school gate. And you go straight on down the hill, and keep on going. And you come to a roundabout, and then the Lollipop Lady helps you across the road, and you keep on going straight down, and there's a road called Priory Road. And you go down till you come to a letterbox, and you go up that Hill Road and 28 and that's my house.

Gavin shows similar features to Karen in his lack of orientation (left and right). But he gives some features of the route. The Lollipop Lady is unlikely to be a permanent landmark, but the roundabout (traffic island) and postbox are. His other advance is to give two street names and the number of his house. If we get lost we shall have the necessary information to make enquiries.

Sandra

> Walk down the hill till you get to the infant school. Then go down the other hill, and then you go down to the roundabout. Go by down to the church, then to the chemist, to the health centre. Then if you walk up from the health centre there's a road going up to the right and a road to the left. Go down to the right – that's Isserley Road, and then there's Hursley Road, and then Salisbury Road. My house is next to Scissors, the hairdresser's.

Sandra is very careful about landmarks – church, health centre, chemist – and the names of streets, and she can use left and right – if the enquirer can get that far – and street names. No house number is given, but we are told it is next to the hairdresser's – which side? (Perhaps there is only one house next to the hairdresser's but we don't know that.)

Mark

> You go down Stokehill Road. There's a pub on the left corner and you turn left and follow Prince Charles Road down to the No Entry Sign. Then you carry on until you come to 33 Prince Charles Road, and that's my house.

Mark is thinking more succinctly than the others. He has no need to go into details of rising or falling ground. The names of the streets give sufficient information – they dispense with the need for topographical details. He indicates the significant landmarks, orients and gives his own address. His is the only set of directions from which we could be sure of arriving at our destination, although his instructions are shorter. It might seem that Mark lived nearer to the school and thus had an easier task. This is not true. His economy just makes it seem so.

Truth and conviction

In Chapter 10 we discussed truth and its validation, and the different forms this validation may take in literal and in imaginative language. In the former, represented by Giving Directions in the present chapter, we are looking for information and validation – details such as landmarks. In the latter – the story-telling – though details and explanations are offered we are much more concerned, as in Helen's piece about the escaped prisoner, with the verisimilitude of the whole, so that we are convinced of its truthfulness. We want it 'realized' – that is 'made real' – before our eyes. And this is what she does with detail, description and enthusiastic presentation. One traditional definition of poetry perhaps best sums up this emotional conviction – 'truth driven alive into the heart by passion'.

14 Short turn development: discussions

ANDREW WILKINSON

Discussion at 7

Young children before they attend school can converse well. Their use of short turns for a variety of social and cognitive processes is developing fast. Their ability to 'argue', for instance, is a case in point. A dispute over a toy with 3-year-olds is by no means always settled by physical means. One child can put a case in favour of having it which includes points from the other child's point of view. We saw this with Cory and Janet in Chapter 2. Hypotheses are offered at concrete level ('If you won't have one, none'). They know the need to validate their statements.

By the age of 7 the children's skills have often widened to include the discussion not only of possessions but also of propositions. In a study by Shea (1988) a peer-group of 7-year-olds was working on a project – building a school for the future. The actual time spent discussing the task was minimal, presumably because the thinking largely went on in their hands as they constructed the buildings from a small crate of Lego Duplo. The initial negotiation was:

James: I'll do a classroom.
Tom: No we we all do a wall to start off with.
James: We have to make the classroom first.
Tom: No we don't, we make the walls first, then we make the classrooms. We put them in and . . .
Tessie: But how are we going to get our hands in?
Tom: We'll put the top on last.

(Shea 1988: 41–2)

This is a jockeying for position in which Tom makes a successful bid for the leadership. Even so he is obliged to provide a rationale for his strategy by explaining in effect that the other processes will be possible because the roof goes on last.

As this work continues over fifty minutes, discussion of the task intermittently occurs amongst social and other talk. Particularly noticeable is this passage which starts on the level of self-aggrandisement and moves into more abstract matters:

Edmund: I know that, Tessie. I know everything, Tessie.
Tessie: No you don't.
Tom: No you don't. Nobody knows everything 'cos in the year 2000.
Tessie: God knows everything.
  (*General laughter*)
James: No he don't.
Tessie: He does because he's got his plans for everything.
Tom: No he doesn't, 'cos he doesn't know that there's going to be a bomb and there's going to be people fall off.
James: Oh, a walk at the edge of the world and fall off . . .
Tom: Yeah, but he doesn't know that there's going to be people fall off the edge of the world. Even God doesn't really know.
Tessie: He does because he's the one who plans to do it.
Tom: God isn't real because I pray to him sometimes and I say please God if you're real make me . . . one of my stickers fall off my wall.
Edmund: It never happens.
James: I know, because he's not there, he's a long way up. You can't whisper to him when he's about 5,000 miles up.
Tessie: You can't really say that 'cos that's not a real prayer, is it? If you say something like Dear God thank you for everything – that's a prayer, that's a prayer.
James: Yeah, he can't listen to us.
  (*Indecipherable noise*)
Edmund: How are you doing up there? He doesn't make any gangs or anything like that. How are you doing up there Fred? How are you doing?
Tom: Fred?
Tessie: Well just because he doesn't make any sound, you don't think . . . some day the world just clashed two pieces together, and . . .
James: God isn't up there you know. He's down there. He's buried.
Tom: That's an argument, and we're not breaking out an argument about God now.

(Shea 1988: 47–8)

These children have *information*. Their knowledge of the world is developing. There is a reference to the possibility of nuclear destruction, and to theories of the origin of the world – 'creation' versus the big bang. Prayer, Tessie thinks, has its own rituals. On the other hand, this knowledge is uncertain: there are the references by two of the children to the possibility of falling off the edge of the world.

This information is not inert – it is used for the *validation* of the points of view expressed. Tessie starts from the point that 'God knows everything'. She is thus in a position to answer James by arguing that you cannot say he doesn't exist because he is silent, and that it is illogical to imagine that the world was not created by him, but by two stars colliding.

> Well just because he doesn't make any sound, you don't think . . . some day the world just clashed two pieces together.

She answers Tom's scepticism about prayer by saying he wasn't using the proper forms:

> You can't really say that 'cos that's not a real prayer, is it? If you say something like Dear God thank you for everything – that's a prayer.

Tom's position denies a prescient god. Tessie asserts it and they are trapped in the free-will/predestination argument which has perplexed theologians for centuries. Tom abandons it and turns to the lack of empirical demonstration of God's existence:

> God isn't real because I pray to him sometimes and I say please God if you're real make me . . . one of my stickers fall off my wall.

Edmund's attack is satirical, calling to 'Fred' who can't possibly hear messages. James thinks he is 5,000 miles up and thus quite naturally cannot hear whispered prayers. But a few lines later he represents him as buried. This may be an inconsistency, or a reference to Christ, though there are reasons for doubting this. In either case the deity is located in space:

> God isn't up there you know. He's down there. He's buried.

Tom's final comment is an *evaluation* of the way the conversation is going:

> That's an argument, and we're not breaking out in an argument about God now.

Tom shows an ability to stand back from the discussion, and comment that it is not relevant to the task in hand. In this sense he *evaluates* it.

The interpersonal aspects of the discussion centre on Tessie's claims about the omniscience of God. She has the leading cognitive role in that she asserts and maintains her position, and rebuts all the criticisms. Tom takes the lead against her. James and Edmund support him, but they each have their own points; also they are not just combating Tessie, but responding to one another. We saw earlier that Tom claimed the leading procedural role; he is aware of the rule of relevance and closes the discussion by tactical means.

The text is coherent because all contributors focus on Tessie's position, and because it is not extended (Tom cuts it off). Even though in places the grammar does not quite make sense ('some day the world just clashed two pieces together') the language is vivid and clear in the crucial words. The high point dramatically is Edmund's humorously irreverent address to 'Fred'.

In another discussion the children were asked to imagine they were shipwrecked and thrown up on a shore somewhere, and to discuss and agree the five most important things they must do in order of importance. There was a minimal initial discussion to set the scene, in which the teacher described the task. This was disposed of expeditiously in fifteen minutes, and they went on to discuss related matters and topics of more interest to them:

Tom:	Bait is something that fish likes . . . they go . . . and you just have to tie some bait . . .
Tessie:	What if there is no bait?
Tom:	Well you wouldn't have a fishing rod and bait, but you could find some bait – just a bit of meat or something like that and you tie it on and you have to get the fish to eat it.
Tessie:	And what if there isn't any sticks?
Tom:	And swallow, then swallow.
Tessie:	Look, no trees, no sticks.
Edmund:	Part of the shipwreck would be a bit of wood.
Tessie:	How do you know that you went on a ship? You might have gone on an aeroplane.
Edmund:	It was a ship.
Tom:	'Cos Mrs Shea said you got . . . it was a shipwreck.
Tessie:	Oh yes, of course. Well maybe all the wood has floated away.
James:	Yes but what if bits of wood have fell on the island.
	(*Confused interjections*)
Tom:	I'm tired of this, Tessie. You're making us have nothing else to do because you're saying 'What if there isn't anything?'.

(Shea 1988: 67–8)

In this situation Tessie takes a provocative negative role and has the boys dancing to her tune, continually challenging them to find answers. The only one she accepts as valid is that supported by authority: Tom says

'Cos Mrs Shea said you got . . . it was a shipwreck

Interestingly Tom withdraws 'you(ve) got (to)'. Perhaps he anticipates 'why?'. In the end the only way he can win is by combating her attitude, not her ideas. This is an evaluation of the situation very similar to the one he made previously. Honours are very evenly distributed between these two.

Much of the dialogue of this group has been unrelated to the task set. Yet the discussion about God is the best part of their 'school-building' session. Children together for long periods – a year, several years – have agendas of importance to them which a classroom discussion, ostensibly on something else, may provide a forum for. They have personal lives of which class is just one aspect (as with Susan in Chapter 6). Three papers in *Oracy Matters* (MacLure *et al.* 1988) have reference to this. Berrill (1988: 57–68) perceives the importance of 'anecdote' to argument. In answer to his own question 'Is there a task in this class?' (11–12 year olds) Halligan (1988: 91–2) comments, 'So there isn't simply a task in the class, there are a large number of them being negotiated, reviewed and revised as the pupils, in coming to terms with one another, come to terms with the few written words which are the official task'. And Phillips (1988: 80) says 'Schools are places where children discover what knowledge is. In school children can become experimenters, explorers and hypothesizers coming at knowledge from the inside, or they can become marketeers trading in knowledge "goods" from a central store in which they have no stake'. These writers are not saying that relevance is not a feature of good argument. Their question is – relevance to what?

A discussion at 11

The differences between the discussions of 7-year-olds and 11-year-olds cannot be described in simple linear terms. So much will depend on the circumstances in which each group is talking, their interrelationships, their knowledge of the topic, the task, their interests and motivation. We shall examine part of a discussion between a group of 11-year-olds on the theme, 'Should parents control the lives of their teenage children?', note its features, and then consider its relationship to that of the 7-year-olds in the previous section.

Sean initiates the discussion, giving a role to both parties:

> I think parents should have some control over their teenage children. Like they should have some control over what kind of clothes you wear. Teenagers should have a bit of control if they want to wear – Joe uses, you know not expensive shirts.

But then, thinking as he talks, he develops this point – teenage choice should not run to extremes:

> but I think you can't go really punk. I think your parents should have some control if you're really punky – you know, spiked, coloured hair, purple hair like um chains, jeans, jackets every day, leather stuff, make up, you got stuff, you know, ugly shoes, pants with holes in them all over.

The basis of this authority of parents, in his view, is their experience:

> Because they've been a teenager, and they probably know what's going on, and what they've done when they were teenagers. Parents know best.

This view is immediately supported by Peter ('Yes, because they've lived a life before') and by Jody ('because they might have been in the same situation when they were young'). Trevor agrees also, but goes on to speak of the parents' feelings and desires:

> They just want you to get a supportive job and go through school so he or her can support a family with nice clothes, houses, food, etc. And also want you to hang around with the right people so you won't pick up bad habits like smoking, or drinking, or drugs. Like say, like Bart said here, like people go around wearing leather jackets and people don't pay attention to them because . . .

Peter supports this last point of Trevor's – the shunning of undesirable companions – 'Yeah, because they'll stay away from him – there's something wrong with him'. But Sean picks up Trevor's first and main point – the effect on the parents of their children's behaviour.

> Like, you I think should have some say because if your kid goes around vandalizing places and killing, like stealing, well that's going to give you a bad name, like the

parents a bad name. Everybody's going to think that the parent did not raise him right or the parent's a dummy.

Trevor is not really listening to Sean. He is following up his own last point about 'bad habits' and he interrupts with

My Dad said if I was taking drugs or something, like, he'd say, 'I'd rather you drank a whole bottle of booze in one shot than take drugs because drugs are more harmful'.

Peter doesn't really want to accept this 'lesser of two evils' argument: 'Well, booze is bad'. Trevor in response merely repeats his statement, and it is left to Peter to draw out the moral about the wages of sin:

Yeah, like you'll just get sick and puke and you'll hate it and you won't do it again.

This phase of the discussion is summed up by Jody in almost traditional phraseology:

I think they should have control over your life because they brought you into this world, and they're your guardian until you move on or something.

This part of the discussion has been concerned with the maintenance of consensus. But the holding up for inspection of the ideas enables Sean to begin to express reservations about the consensus. In reply to Jody he asks what arises if the parents' control becomes unacceptable:

I don't think so. That's like, that's why some kids run away, because they don't like the way their parents treat them.

He gets support from Peter, but Jody objects that they are 'talking about a normal parent', and when the others jeer at this he repeats his formulation:

Your parents brought you into the world and they'd probably be more than happy to bring you out of it (support you?).

But Trevor warns that even such parents can deteriorate:

And like some of your parents they ask you to do everything. Hey kid, can you go to the store and get me a bag of milk and some cig? Then they give them ten bucks to spend at the store for himself. That's all right but . . . but if they keep asking you like maybe every day or something to do it going to be a habit. Like people won't like him because he's too lazy.

Peter, who has murmured an objection at Trevor's 'That's all right . . .' now comes in with

Even one cigarette is like, even one cigarette can ruin your life.

From this, and the way the group takes up the point, it is clear that they have a shared understanding, not explicit in the text, that the reward money will be spent on cigarettes.

This sets the group off at a tangent on the addictiveness of tobacco, and the morality of the farmers who grow it. Trevor is making a contribution to this when he suddenly realizes it's not on the official agendum.

> Yeah, that's because people from Canada come into the United States and buy. . . . What are we supposed to be talking about?

Sean, who has remained silent during the digression, comes in in a tone of exaggerated restraint:

> Let me say something, OK? We're sure taking one point and making that point to another point, and making that point to another point, and talk about that point.

Jenny, the only girl in the group, has for some time said nothing. It's as though she is waiting until all the preliminaries are out of the way so that serious discussion can begin. She now comes in, referring for the first time to the extract they were given to prompt the discussion:

> Okay, in the play I think the parents should let the teenager take the job because, I mean the parent would want the teenager to become independent, and know what a job is like. And . . .

She attempts to introduce the topic of independence in the context of the play, but the boys do not follow it up, instead discussing anecdotally the age (14 or 16) at which it is possible to be employed. After some twenty exchanges, when Peter says: 'You can be six to get a job, you get a paper route it's still a job', Jenny comes back with a slightly impatient patience:

> Yes, but that's not the point.

Sean now supports her, referring once again to the situation in the extract:

> Yes, it's not the point. As it refers in this play, this kid has got a job. Now I think he should have asked his parents before doing that.

Now the way is open for a serious discussion of the issues. Tevor introduces the matter of bad companions:

> *Trevor:* Right, in this play the parent doesn't think the teenager should get this job because he doesn't like who he'd be working with.
> *Jenny:* Not who he'd be working with – the people in the . . .
> *Peter:* The people who he'd be hanging around with. They could be drinking and smoking.
> *Jody:* The parent has warned the teenager in this play that if, like, he got this job he or she would be hanging around.
> *Jenny:* Yes, but the job he or she is taking has something to do with the class she or he is taking.

Trevor recapitulates. Jenny insists he be accurate – it's not the workmates but the hangers on who are the danger – but reminds the group that the work has a relationship to the course (presumably meaning that there will be motivation not to waste time).

The discussion continues and develops to a consideration of short-term and long-term objectives:

Jody: Now with all this practising that means it's probably going to ruin this kid's life, and after every work job at night he's going to be practising for his examination. When he could if he didn't have this job and went to school (*i.e. college*) maybe get a better job after he went to school (*college*).

Trevor: If he got that job then I think his parents are right, because if he got that job he might not want to have it any more, and then he can't get a better job or something. He needs a good education.

Peter: But he's already got a good education.

Trevor: Yeah, but he'll have to go back to school (*college*) to get his diploma.

Peter: But he'll already have it.

Trevor: No because it says you have to pass the examination.

And Trevor validates his remark by reference back to the text.

A comparison of the two discussions

It will be useful to look at some features of these two discussions – at 7 and at 11 – in terms set out in the Assessment Model (see p. 123).

Ideational (what is said)

Cognition

With the 7-year-olds there is principally a concern with 'describing' (offering facts and assertions) and interpreting. In the discussion about God, for example, they are making assertions and supporting them by reasons. There is, however, speculation in the boys' proposals about the desert island and in Tessie's rejection of them. With the 11-year-olds the earlier sections are 'descriptive' (again offering facts and assertions), but the discussion moves to speculation arising from the extract.

The question is not whether such mental processes such as description, interpretation and speculation occur, but the level at which they occur. And this is where we need to consider the quality of information, of validation, and of evaluation.

The information the 7-year-olds have in their discussion about God is remarkable: as we have seen there is reference to the possibility of nuclear destruction and to theories of creation. They use this for validation of their arguments, and again we looked above at the range of validations they used. The characteristic of their information and validation is that on the whole it consists of things they have been told, whereas that of the 11-year-olds is from things they have observed or experienced. They have learned to use evidence, as provided by the text they were initially given. On the whole the younger children do not evaluate their own offerings, but the older children several times revise in the course of a sentence ('if your kid goes around vandalizing places and killing, like stealing', i.e. 'I mean stealing, not killing'). The evaluation by the younger children of one another's offerings tends to be completely supportive or completely contradictory. ('I know everything, Tessie' – 'No, you don't'.) The older children often tend to accept one another's utterances but modify them ('He needs a good education' – 'But he's already got a good education'). Both groups, or at least individuals in them, show an ability to evaluate the group performance. In the younger group it is Tom who brings it back to the agenda ('That's an argument, and we're not breaking out in an argument about God now'), and also criticizes Tessie's negative strategy ('You're making us have nothing else to do because you are saying what if there isn't anything'). In the older group Jenny is the person who is monitoring the group as well as participating in its activities, and she does this over long stretches of text. She merely listens in the first two phases, but initiates the third, and keeps it on track when it seems to wander again ('Yes, but that's not the point'). Perhaps her detachment comes because she is the only girl in the group.

Affect

Awareness of other people and their needs is a feature of the older group. They speculate, not only about the teenager in the extract, with whom they could reasonably be expected to identify, but also about the feelings of parents, and the effects of a delinquent son on them. The younger children do not display this, but this is not to be taken as a criticism – their topic of discussion did not provide opportunity for it.

Interpersonal (how it is said)

Roles

In the younger group Tom immediately assumes the leadership. And in fact he maintains it, in both the building of the school and the organizing of the discussion. But equally dominant as far as the argument is concerned is Tessie, who takes on all the boys repeatedly, and is brought to a halt only by Tom's use of the rules of procedure. No child plays a passive role – all are co-operative in the sense of contributing ideas to the discussion. Edmund's unique contribution is of a comedy act.

With the older group there is no conflict in personal terms: nothing parallel to Tessie's combat with the boys. It is the ideas that are important. And there is no single dominant person, though Stephen and Jody contribute more ideas. Jenny's contribution is accepted and made use of on its merits and not because of her sex (the use of 'he or she' to refer back to the 'he' in the extract is interesting). Participants move in and out of leading roles. Jenny's contribution is particularly useful: she spends a lot of time listening, and on the whole does not say much, but no one does more to influence the course of the discussion.

Rules

Both groups are aware of the main rules of discussion. The older group listen more to what everyone has to say instead of filling the silence immediately as do the younger group, but even with this group there is appropriate turn-taking. The older group is far more concerned to produce consensus, and in the first two phases members agree with one another to an excessive degree. The younger group are less concerned with consensus and more with leadership. Even so the rules are observed in seeking it. It is only when Tom uses a procedural device to close part of the discussion unattractive to him that we see the rules being used other than for the pursuit of the ideas concerned.

Presentation

In group discussion presentation is far less apparent than in story-telling or exposition to a group of listeners. Other participants often (but by no means always) look at the speaker. Speakers often look at the group generally (but not at individuals) when they talk. Sometimes they talk meditatively with their eyes down – and the older group did this a good deal. It seemed to the observer to be a way of objectifying the issues.

Textual (*the form chosen*)

The structure of the first conversation of the younger children is not related to the task they have been set. Nevertheless it has a coherence about it since it focuses on the arguments for and against the existence of God. It is questionable how long this could have carried on had it not been terminated. The older group had, as was to be expected, an ability to sustain discussion over longer stretches, a sense of where it was going, and how it could be extended. They were able to work to a brief, even though they at times digressed from it.

The lexis and idioms display many differences between the two groups. The statements of the younger are unambiguous and assertive ('God knows everything.' 'No he don't.'). Those of the older are marked by tentativeness: for instance, by 'I think' (i.e. take it for what it's worth); by 'you know' (an appeal for support); by 'like' (usually introducing an example or redefinition to support a statement which might seem too unqualified). Again, as far as stylistic flourishes are concerned, there is no parallel to Edmund's apostrophe to the Deity in the older group. But Sean provides a very vivid description of a 'real punk':

> if you're really punky – you know, spiked, coloured hair, purple hair like um chains, jackets every day, leather stuff, make-up, you got stuff, you know, ugly shoes, pants with holes in them all over.

But it is important to realize that this passage is not there for its stylistic features but as a validation of Sean's point about the kind of clothing which would be properly unacceptable to parents.

A question of development

Can we point to 'developmental' features in the older group as distinct from the younger? The younger group confront one another, the older group seek consensus; the younger group are absolute in their opinions, the older are more tentative; the younger group use knowledge they have been told, the older validate much more on their own experience of the real world, and can use evidence; members of the older group are more likely to listen to others, and to restrain comment till an appropriate time; the older group can operate far longer stretches of discussion, they are more aware of its progress, and their sense of relevance to the brief is greater. In the younger group the girl and the boys are at odds; in the older group both sexes are listened to for their contributions. Of course some of the differences between the two groups are due to differences of task and context, and perhaps to the fact that the younger are British, the older Canadian. There is a good deal that we can reasonably consider developmental. Even so there is a large age gap (four years) between the two groups, so we would expect this. Such differences are by no means the same as the fine discriminations implied in the Cox Report (DES 1988b; 1989) the search for which could easily distort the assessment process. We may repeat the words with which we opened Chapter 13. Language development obviously takes place, but it does not take place obviously.

PART FIVE
Listen carefully

Oracy involves both speaking and listening. Research demonstrates that listening is not as efficient a function as it may be but this is not to say that we need 'listening programmes' specifically to train it in isolation from other activities. There are three reasons for considering it. The first is that it is through listening that we acquire our own language, and the particular registers we need for all kinds of speech. Whether deliberately or accidentally, society is constantly provided speech models. In school we may do this deliberately; we may require the production on tape of a radio programme which requires the different registers and styles of news reader, commentator, interviewer, reader of poetry or short story, actor in a radio drama.

The second reason is that listening may be the basis for an exciting study of language in action, whose source materials can be obtained on tape from broadcasting and actuality. Corresponding to the literary classics one would look for radio plays, programmes, and speeches where the spoken mode is used creatively. One thinks, for instance, of Louis MacNeice's *Dark Tower*, or the *Big Hewer* and other radio ballads, produced by Charles Parker. But one would also concern oneself with questions about the language of young children, the language of the pop world, or advertising, the use of ambiguities by politicians, the differences between standard and non-standard speech, the accents of English and English-speaking peoples, the functions of different registers, the breaking of register, the nature of cliché and jargon. A radio interview can be evaluated in terms of the completeness or otherwise of the questions asked, and whether they are answered or not. More difficult work would explore the nature of our understanding of the spoken language. One might for instance give part of a conversation – ask what came before, and what is likely to follow – and what clues there are which enable one to do this. It seems likely that the ability to make such predictions is an important part of understanding – the questions of what is good speech implied in this paper can be considered. How are pauses being used? How far is 'fluency' synonymous with oracy?

The third reason for mentioning listening is for what it implies about human relationships. One sometimes finds children (and adults too) whose monologues show no concern for the listener or his point of view. If there were no other reason for emphasizing it, listening would still be an essential component of oracy, for it implies respect for the other person as a person.

(Wilkinson 1968: 74)

May I now turn to listening, because if speaking is neglected, listening is unheard of in common educational practice. The new linguistics, I think, has contributed a great deal to our knowledge of the spoken language, and has modified our attitudes towards it. It has much to contribute to our teaching but not the sort of contribution that some people are suggesting it should make in English schools. I would be very suspicious of formal grammatical training derived from the new linguistics, or anything resembling it, but the spoken language I think is a field in which we can interest children in language. There's a magnificent passage in the preface to that great 1765 dictionary of Samuel Johnson. He's talking about the words he has put in and the words he has left out and, quite clearly, he's not very enthusiastic about certain words. These are the words which he dubs in his dictionary *low* or *mean* or *barbarous* or *bad*. It is very interesting that many of them are spoken and not written words. Here is the passage.

> That many terms of art and manufacture are omitted, must be frankly acknowledged; but for this defect I may boldly allege that it was unavoidable: I could not visit caverns to learn the miner's language, nor take a voyage to perfect my skill in the dialect of navigation, nor visit the warehouses of merchants, and shops of artificers to gain the name of wares, tools, and operations, of which no mention is found in books; what favourable accident or easy enquiry brought within my reach, has not been neglected, but it had been a hopeless labour to glean up words by courting living information, and contesting with the sullenness of one, and the roughness of another.

What does Johnson mean by courting living information? He means that he is not going to listen to words as they are on the tongues of men, nor to have words which are not found in books, nor to listen to living speech. Johnson was deaf, and he hadn't time. What he did do was a monument, and he was anyway within the assumptions of his age. But we are not any longer bound by those assumptions. What I am saying is that listening in schools could be made fascinating by providing what Johnson called 'living information', by providing tapes and records and perhaps videotapes of the spoken language. In England there are radio plays, in both countries there are records available; but more there are tape recorders. We have the ability to get conversations down on tape or to make conversations, to put specially on tape, to record different dialects, different idiolects, to ask questions about the difference between the spoken and the written language, to ask questions about the sorts of relationships which are going on as expressed through language.

What we want in the listening field is 'living information', and I think the time is right, both in the United Kingdom and in America, for the construction of a new spoken literature (the word *literature* is question begging), a new body of 'living information' which will motivate our children, including the less able children who are not terribly interested in books but who are listening and speaking all the time.

(Wilkinson 1970: 76–7)

15 'Living information'

ANDREW WILKINSON

Listening is most acute when it is purposeful – in a conversation when we have to respond or silence and embarrassment ensue, or at a public meeting when we are going to question the speaker and wish to make sure we have got the point. The Cox Report says 'although there are some widespread non-reciprocal speaking and listening situations (such as radio, television, public address systems and lectures) the processes of listening and speaking are primarily reciprocal and integrated' (DES 1989: 15.53). This may be true. The difficulty is that these widespread situations are frequently the ones in which powerful people try to influence or manipulate us. This passage of Cox needs to be taken alongside another, which speaks of how, through the media, teenagers will see and hear an abundance of information which they will need to evaluate and use judiciously for their own purposes. . . . As potential jurors or witnesses, voters or representatives of political or interest groups, they will need to know how to judge or present a spoken case, how to recognize emotive language and arguments that are specious or selective, and how to marshal facts with clarity and precision (DES 1989: 15.7).

Listening in these circumstances cannot be passive. A recording of a radio or television interview is listened to for the purposes of discussing it, analysing it, writing about it, and so on. We proposed one possible scheme of analysis of such material based on the sentence WHO communicates WHAT, to WHOM, HOW and WHY, and on WHAT OCCASION? It is not appropriate to develop these terms here but they are explained and their use illustrated by examples in *The Quality of Listening* (Wilkinson *et al.* 1974: 66–76).

We suggested in the original *Spoken English* (Wilkinson 1965) that a school should build up a library of sound tapes (we would now include video tapes) of 'living information', to employ Johnson's term, for study and other use. In the passage quoted at the beginning of this chapter we suggested some of the possible items. Others would be notable speeches – Churchill's wartime broadcasts, Martin Luther King's 'I have a dream' – so that the vision of greatness is not lost sight of. Yet others would be family stories and histories: the accession of the mini-recorder has made the production of good recordings by pupils themselves a possibility.

Listening log

This idea, suggested by Deborah Berrill, was implemented by students on a Summer School at the University of British Columbia (UBC) in the summer of 1988, taught by Andrew Wilkinson. These students were in fact mature teachers, but there is no reason in principle why the same sort of log could not be kept by teenagers and perhaps younger people.

The idea is to net the spoken word as it flies, pin it down on paper, and make an appropriate entry about it. The captured words do not have to be dazzlingly beautiful: they can be very boring in content as long as they have interest as language. Some times a mini-recorder might be available, but often it is only when one is miles from any such resource that the butterfly flutters before one's eyes. Hence it becomes an exercise in exact memory. The teachers found their ears atuned, in a way they would never have thought possible, to the sounds going on around them. The comments were not required to be long but they had to explain why this particular specimen was worthy of capture.

There follow several examples – a short anthology of 'living information' – to close the book.

First, a conversation between two doctors who are examining my knee. They make no effort to share the information with me until I interrupt.

First doctor: The MEL shows signs of rotational stretching – try the 30% turn.
Second doctor: The lateral is definitely torn, and I don't see any evidence of that.
Patient: You mean my crucial ligaments are damaged?
Second doctor: (*slightly supercilious*) Cruciate ligaments actually.
First doctor: But they sure are crucial all right.

The technical language is a register of authority for some. The second doctor is a trainee who has not yet identified himself as such. He is quick to correct my excursion into his territory. The other doctor perceives the snub, however, and tries to make amends for it.   (PB)

Second, a young woman speaking on the telephone smiles when saying, 'Oh hello Grandma, is Dad there?', and then ceases to smile.

This non-linguistic behaviour is interesting since it occurs in the absence of an addressee. It is a comment on the power of acoustic stimulus. Is there a natural reluctance to forgo the richness of context that we associate with oral discourse? Does the physical act of smiling alter the character of the speech, or was it simply an involuntary reaction to hearing the voice of a loved one? As a postscript I have seen my Japanese-Canadian mother-in-law actually bow down while speaking on the phone.   (RM)

Third, at the fruit market, background noise commercial from a radio backed by music. Man (50s) and woman (40s) stand in line to pay. They do not know each other; they are talking about their children, and specifically about the ages of the woman's three children (8, 10, 22).

> *Man:* Nothing like spacing them out. This is my baby. (*He points to a 200-lb girl of around 20 years old*)
> *Woman:* They grow up fast, don't they?

You could cut the embarrassment with a knife, it was so thick. Both the man's and woman's comments were a desperate attempt at continuing a 'waiting-in-line' conversation. I thought that they each 'Put their foot in the mouth' and obviously they thought so too – I could see the thoughts racing through their minds. This is a common feature of an on-the-spot conversation between two strangers. Under the pressure to respond they say embarrassing or meaningless things just to have something to say.   (BVA)

Fourth, on a garbage container a third word has been added to the two stencilled on it, obviously by a visiting teacher.

> *She:* Is that a garbage container?
> *He:* Yes, of course it is.
> *She:* But why have they written on it?
> *He:* What?
> *She:* Look (*reads*) No Paint, No Bottles, No Principles.
> *He:* Well, I don't see why they should exclude Principals. I've known a few that that would've been the best place for them.
> (*Laughter; he takes her hand*)

This was fascinating because neither of them appeared to have noticed the misspelling of the crucial word. Or perhaps they had and were both sharing the pun without remarking on it. At any rate this incident demonstrates how the word created closeness in shared laughter.   (RB)

Fifth, a phone call: I wanted to speak to a gentleman on the phone but he was not at home. A guest was in the house who said he would find me a number where I could reach him.

> *Guest:* Just a minute . . . um . . . I'll see if I can find you a number . . . so you can phone . . . Wendy! What's Martin's office number? My wife . . . if you can bear with me . . . I'm looking through my business cards . . . um . . . now . . . there . . . OK I found it, his number is 617382.

This man I was speaking to was concerned to keep contact with me, by giving a running commentary on his actions, by explaining what he was doing to me (calling to his wife). He obviously felt the lack of a face-to-face situation and was trying to substitute for it.   (GS)

Sixth, party talk: two women talking to John, a coroner, about language used amongst coroners.

Mary: How do you talk about those dead bodies?

John: If it's been a fire victim we call them crispy critters – that's the word they use – or you get a guy that was a swinger – someone that hung himself. Then you get people that have blown their heads off because of their state of mind – they just lose it. We find that more men take their lives through violent means – women would take it through alcohol or drugs and things like that, just mellow out on carbon monoxide.

Mary: How local is crispy critters?

John: Probably universal. Yes, you were asking how do you deal with it. It's not that we become hardened to it, or that you get callous. I look at it with the attitude that it's no longer a human being. The life is gone, basically it's just a body there.

Mary: The person's not there any more.

John: The time that it bothers me is children.

Denise: I've heard that. The thing that I think about these nicknames is that it has much more to do with a shared experience than a hardening. I mean, teachers refer to kids as noudges.

Mary: Noudges – what's that?

Denise: You know, someone who (*makes a motion of tugging her*). Yiddish word. So there are certain characteristics that are character types in any environment, and eventually you are able to coin a phrase, so that you can key into somebody else's experience. I think you can make an argument that's hardening, but I see it much more as a key thing about the camaraderie that goes on in any environment.

John is furnishing information about a register familiar to him but not to us. The words evoke stories for him which he went on to share with us, thereby enhancing relationships since we found this insightful, and sought reasons and explanations for the use of these terms. Denise's point about shared experience has validity; through language we establish empathy with others and these private registers can have a unifying effect for an entire group without much else being said. Such a register can easily be not understood, misunderstood, or judged by others.

(SH)

Finally, a conversation with a phone canvasser.

KS: Hello, Mr Bird?

PB: Yes.

KS: My name is Ken Smithson, and I'm from Mount Pleasant Carpet Cleaning, and how are you today sir?

PB: Mediocre.

KS: That's good sir. We are going to be in your neighbourhood, and would like to offer you our summer special on sitting room and dining room. Would you be interested?

PB: No.

KS: Thank you.

Canvassing is a hard job which must eventually lead to conversational disfunction. His lack of reaction to my response shows that this conversation is not interactive until the bait of the proposed service is offered.   (PB)

Items contributed by Paul Bird, Roberta Bramwell, Sabina Harpe, Gun Shah and Benita Van Andel.

Bibliography

Abercrombie, D. (1963) 'Conversation and spoken prose', *English Language Teaching*, 18, 1, reprinted in D. Abercrombie (1965) *Studies in Phonetics and Linguistics*, Oxford, Oxford University Press.

Andrews, R. (ed.) (1990) *Narrative and Argument*, Milton Keynes, Open University Press.

APU (Assessment of Performance Unit) (1984) *Language Performance in Schools. 1982 Secondary survey report*, London, Department of Education and Science.

Atkinson, D. (1965) 'A test of listening comprehension for the Certificate of Secondary Education', unpublished report to the Schools Council.

Barnes, D. (1976) *From Communication to Curriculum*, Harmondsworth, Penguin.

Barnes, D. and Todd, F. (1977) *Communication and Learning in Small Groups*, London, Routledge & Kegan Paul.

Barnes, D., Britton, J. N. and Rosen, H. (1971) *Language, the Learner, and the School*, Harmondsworth, Penguin.

Barnes, D., Britton, J. L. and Torbe, M. (1986) *Language, the Learner and the School*, 3rd edn, Harmondsworth, Penguin.

Berger, P. L. and Kellner, H. (1964) 'Marital conversation and the construction of reality', *Diogenes*, Vol. 46, No. 1.

Berger, P. L. and Luckman, J. (1967) *The Social Construction of Reality*, Harmondsworth, Penguin.

Berrill, D. P. (1988) 'Anecdote and the development of oral argument in sixteen-year-olds', in M. MacLure, T. Phillips and A. M. Wilkinson (eds) *Oracy Matters*, Milton Keynes, Open University Press.

Boomer, G. (1983) 'Oracy in Australian Schools', *English in Australia*, 13, 3.

Bremner, J. G. (1984) *Infancy*, Oxford, Basil Blackwell.

British Columbia Student Assessment (1988) *Enhancing and Evaluating Oral Communication in the Intermediate Grades*, Ministry of Education, British Columbia.

Britton, J. N. (1986) 'Talking to learn', in D. Barnes, J. Britton, and M. Torbe, *Language, the Learner and the School*, 3rd edn, Harmondsworth, Penguin.

Britton, J. N., Burgess, T., Martin, N., McLeod, A., and Rosen, H. (1973) *The Development of Writing Abilities*, London, Macmillan Education.

Brooks, G. (1987) *Speaking and Listening Assessment at Age 15*, Windsor, NFER-Nelson.

Brown, G. and Yule, G. (1983) *Discourse Analysis*, Cambridge, Cambridge University Press.

Brown, G., Anderson, A., Shillcock, R., and Yule, G. (1984) *Teaching Talk, Strategies for Production and Assessment*, Cambridge, Cambridge University Press.

Bruner, J. (1986) *Actual Minds, Possible Worlds*, Cambridge, Mass., Harvard University Press.

Bullock Report (1975) *A Language for Life*, London, HMSO.

Carré, C. (1981) *Language Teaching and Learning. 4. Science*, London, Ward Lock Educational.

Cavanagh, G. and Styles, K. (1987) 'Criteria for improving small group discussion: evaluating individual effectiveness', HO at Trent University Seminar, Peterborough, Ontario.

Coates, J. (1986) *Women, Men and Language*, London, Longman.

Coates, R. (1982) 'How standard is standard?', in T. Pateman (ed.) *Languages for Life*, University of Sussex, Brighton.

Condon, W. S. and Sander. W. (1974) 'Neonate movement is synchronised with adult speech', *Science*, 183.

Cornwell, P. (1979) 'Group discussion as a language strategy in the primary school', *Language for Learning*, 1, 1, Language in Education Centre, University of Exeter School of Education.

Crystal, D. (1986) *Listen to Your Child*, Harmondsworth, Penguin.

Crystal, D. (1987) *The Cambridge Encyclopedia of Language*, Cambridge, Cambridge University Press.

'Crowther Report' (1959) *15–18*, vol. 1. London, HMSO.

Davies, A. (1973) 'Spoken and written language', Radio Unit 4 for Open University Course, Reading Development, PE951.

Davies, A. (1978) 'Textbook situations and idealised language', *Work in Progress*, 11: 129–33, Department of Linguistics, University of Edinburgh.

Davies, A. (1984) 'Idealisation in sociolinguistics; the choice of of the standard dialect', in D. Schiffrin (ed.) *Meaning, Form and Use in Context: Linguistic Applications*, Washington, DC, Georgetown University Press.

DES (Department of Education and Science) (1988a) *Report of the Committee of Enquiry into the Teaching of English Language*, Kingman Report, London, HMSO.

Department of Education and Science DES, (1988b) *English for Ages 5–11*, the first Cox Report, London, HMSO.

DES (Department of Education and Science), (1989) *English for Ages 5 to 16*, the second Cox Report, National Curriculum Council, 15–17 New Street, York, YO1 2RA.

Dixon, J. and Stratta, L. (1986) 'Argument and the teaching of English; a critical analysis', in A. M. Wilkinson (ed.) 'Aspects of English Composition', *Educational Review*, 38, 2.

Donaldson, M. (1978) *Children's Minds*, London, Fontana.

Dunn, J. (1988) *The Beginnings of Social Understanding*, Oxford, Basil Blackwell.

Edwards, A. D. and Westgate, D. P. C. (1987) *Investigating Classroom Talk*, London and Philadelphia, Pa, Falmer Press.

Eisenberg, A. and Garvey, C. (1981) 'Children's use of verbal strategies in resolving conflicts', *Discourse Processes*, 4: 149–70.

Ellis, R. (1985) *Understanding Second Language Acquisition*, Oxford, Oxford University Press.

Farrar, R. and Richmond, J. (eds) (1979) *How Talking is Learning*, London, ILEA Learning Materials Service.

Finnegan, R. (1988) *Literacy and Orality*, Oxford, Basil Blackwell.

Fox, J. and Pringle, I. (1988) 'Screening Package. The oral language portfolio. Draft material for the senior English Ontario Assessment Instrument Pool, Working Paper. Centre for Applied Language Studies, Carleton University, Ottawa.

French, P. and MacLure, M. (eds) (1981) *Adult–Child Conversation*, London, Croom Helm.

Garvey, C. (1984) *Children's Talk*, Oxford, Fontana.

Goody, J. (1987) *The Interface Between the Written and the Oral*, Cambridge, Cambridge University Press.

Gorman, T. P., White, J. and Brooks, G. (1984) *Language Performance in Schools: 1982 Secondary Survey Report*, London, Department of Education and Science.

Greif, E. B. (1980) 'Sex differences in parent–child conversations', in C. Kramarae (ed.) *The Voices and Words of Women and Men*, Oxford, Pergamon.

Grice, H. P. (1975) 'Logic and Conversation', in P. Cole and J. L. Morgan (eds) *Speech Acts*, New York, Academic Press, pp. 41–58.

Halliday, M. A. K. (1970) 'Language structure and language function', in J. Lyons (ed.) *New Horizons in Linguistics*, Harmondsworth, Penguin.

Halligan, D. (1988) 'Is there a task in this class?' in M. MacLure, T. Phillips and A. M. Wilkinson (eds) *Oracy Matters*, Milton Keynes, Open University Press.

Harris, N. (1989) 'Living history', in Newsletter Issue no. 3. Cheshire Oracy Project, Cheshire Language Centre, North Cheshire College, Padgate Campus, Fearnhead, Warrington, WA2 0DB.

Helm, J. (ed.) (1967) *Essays in the Verbal and Visual Arts*, Seattle, NJ, University of Washington Press.

Herbert, A. J. (1965) *The Structure of Technical English*, London, Longman.

Honey, J. (1983) *The Language Trap*, Kay-Shuttlesworth Papers on Education no. 3, Kenton, Middlesex, National Council for Educational Standards.

Johnson, J. (1988) 'Making talk work', Oracy Issues no. 1, Newsletter of the National Oracy Project, 45 Newcombe House, Notting Hill Gate, London, W11 3JB.

Joos, M. (1962) *The Five Clocks*, The Hague, Mouton.

Kernan, K. (1977) 'Semantic and expressive elaboration in children's narratives', in S. Ervine-Tripp and C. Mitchell-Kernan (eds) *Child Discourse*, New York, Academic Press.

Keynes, G. (ed.) (1956) *Poetry and Prose of William Blake*, London, Nonesuch Press.

Labov, W. (1977) *Language in the Inner City: Studies in the Black English Vernacular*, Oxford, Basil Blackwell.

Labov, W. and Waletsky, J. (1967) 'Narrative analysis: oral versions of personal experience', in J. Helm (ed.) *Essays in the Verbal and Visual Arts*, Seattle, NJ, University of Washington Press.

Lowth, R. (1762) *A Short Introduction to English Grammar*, reissued 1967, London, Menston Scolar Press.

Lyons, J. (1977) *Semantics*, Cambridge, Cambridge University Press.

Macaulay, R. and Trevelyan, G. (1975) *Language, Education, and Employment*, Edinburgh, Edinburgh University Press.

MacLure, M. (1988) 'Assessing spoken language: testing times for talk', in N. Mercer (ed.) *Language and Literacy from an Educational Perspective*, vol. 2, Milton Keynes, Open University Press.

MacLure, M. and French, P. (1981) 'A comparison of talk at home and at school', in G. Wells (ed.) *Learning through Interaction*, Cambridge, Cambridge University Press.

MacLure, M., Phillips, T., and Wilkinson, A. M. (eds) (1988) *Oracy Matters*, Milton Keynes, Open University Press.

McTear, M. (1985) *Children's Conversation*, Oxford, Basil Blackwell.

Marland, M. (1983) *Sex Differentiation and Schooling*, London, Heinemann.

Meek, M., Warlow, A. and Barton, G. (eds) (1977) *The Cool Web: The Pattern of Children's Reading*, London, Bodley Head.

Mercer, N. (ed.) (1988) *Language and Literacy from an Educational Perspective*, vol. 2, Milton Keynes, Open University Press.

Moffett, J. (1968) *Teaching the Universe of Discourse*, Boston, Mass., Houghton Mifflin.

Mowbray, G. (1987) *Speaking Aloud – Allowed*, Curriculum Guidelines, Ministry of Education, Ontario.

NCC (National Curriculum Council) (1989) *A Framework for the Primary Curriculum. Curriculum Guidance 1*, 15–17 New Street, York, YO1 2RA.

National Oracy Project (1988) *Telling Stories in School*, Occasional Papers in Oracy, no. 1, National Oracy Project, Newcombe House, 45 Notting Hill Gate, London, W11 3JB.

Newson, J. and Newson, E. (1975) 'Intersubjectivity and the transmission of culture: on the secret origins of symbolic functioning', *Journal of the British Psychological Society*, Bulletin 28.

Paley, V. G. (1984) *Boys and Girls: Superheroes in the Dolls' Corner*, Chicago, Ill., University of Chicago Press.

Paskin, P. D. (1986) 'A study of group talk, problem solving in a science task', a course study for the Advanced Certificate of Education, University of East Anglia.

Peel, E. A. (1971) *The Nature of Adolescent Judgment*, London, Styles Press.

Phillips, T. (1985) 'Beyond lip service: discourse development after the age of nine', in G. Wells and J. Nicholls (eds) *Language and Learning: An Interactional Perspective*, London and Philadelphia, Pa, Falmer Press.

Phillips, T. (1988) 'On a related matter: why "successful" small group talk depends on not keeping to the point', in M. MacLure, T. Phillips and A. M. Wilkinson (eds) *Oracy Matters*, Milton Keynes, Open University Press.

Piaget, J. and Inhelder, B. (1969) *The Psychology of the Child*, trans. H. Weaver, London, Routledge & Kegan Paul.

Popper, K. R. and Eccles, J. C. (1981) *The Self and its Brain*, New York, Springer International.

Pringle, I. and Fox, J. (1987), 'Assessment of Oral English. Working paper, Centre for Applied Language Studies', Carleton University, Ottawa.

Robinson, R. G. (1988) 'The roles taken in small teacherless groups, and the assessment of those roles', dissertation submitted in part fulfilment of the requirements for the MA degree in the University of East Anglia, Norwich, UK.

Sapir, E. (1960) *Culture, Language and Personality; Selected Essays*, Berkeley, Calif., University of California Press.

Schaffer, H. R. (1974) 'Behavioural synchrony in infancy', *New Scientist*, 62: 16–18.

Scribner, S. and Cole, M. (1981) *The Psychology of Literacy*, Cambridge, Mass., and London, Harvard University Press.

Self, D. (1987) *Listen, Talk, Communicate*, London, Macmillan Education.

Shea, G. (1987) 'A study of gender differences in the language of young children talking in the classroom', paper for the degree of MA, University of East Anglia, Norwich, UK.

Shea, G. (1988) 'The study of language interaction in small groups of seven-year-olds', dissertation for the degree of MA in the University of East Anglia, Norwich, UK.

156   SPOKEN ENGLISH ILLUMINATED

Sinclair, J. McH. and Coulthard, M. (1975) *Towards an Analysis of Discourse*, Oxford, Oxford University Press.

Skull, J. and Wilkinson, A. M. (1969) 'The construction of an oral composition quality scale', *British Journal of Educational Psychology*, 39, 3.

Sokoloff, L. (1989) 'And so to tape', *The Oracle*, 1, 11, Croydon Oracy Project, Davidson Centre, Davidson Road, Croydon, Surrey.

Spender, D. (ed.) (1982) *Invisible Woman: The School Scandal*, London, Chameleon Press.

Stratta, L., Dixon, J. and Wilkinson, A. M. (1973) *Patterns of Language*, London, Heinemann Educational.

Street, B. V. (1984) *Literacy in Theory and Practice*, Cambridge Studies on Oral and Literate Cultures 9, Cambridge, Cambridge University Press.

Sutcliffe, D. (1982) *Black British English*, Oxford, Basil Blackwell.

Sutherland, M. (1981) *Sex Bias in Education*, Oxford, Basil Blackwell.

Tannen, D. and Saville-Troike, M. (eds) (1985) *Perspectives on Silence*, Norwood, NJ, Ablex Publishing.

Tarleton, R. (1988) *Learning and Talking: A Practical Guide to Oracy Across the Curriculum*, London, Routledge.

Thornley-Hall, C. (1988) *Let's Talk about Talk*. An introduction to the Peel Project, Talk, a Medium for Learning and Change. Peel Board of Education, H. J. A. Brown Education Centre, 5650 Hurontario Street, Mississauga, Ontario, L5R 1C6, Canada.

Tizzard, B. and Hughes, M. (1984) *Young Children Learning*, London, Fontana.

Trevarthen, C. (1969) 'Communication and co-operation in early infancy – a description of primary subjectivity', in M. Bullowa (ed.) *Before Speech: The Beginnings of Interpersonal Communication*, Cambridge, Cambridge University Press.

Trudgill, P. (1975) *Accent, Dialect and the School*, London, Edward Arnold.

Trudgill, P. (1983) *On Dialect*, Oxford, Basil Blackwell.

Wade, B. (1985) 'Intervening in Talk', in 'Talking to some purpose', *Educational Review*, Occasional Publication no. 12, University of Birmingham School of Education.

Warburg, J. (1961) 'Notions of correctness', Supplement no. 11 in R. Quirk, *The Use of English*, London, Longman.

Wells, G. (1985) *Language Development in the Pre-School Years*, Cambridge, Cambridge University Press.

Wells, G. (1987) *The Meaning Makers*, London, Hodder & Stoughton.

Wells, G. and Montgomery, M. (1981) 'Adult–Child interaction at home and in school', in P. French and M. MacLure (eds) (1981) *Adult–Child Conversation*, London, Croom Helm.

Wells, G. and Nicholls, J. (eds) (1985) *Language and Learning: An Interactional Perspective*, London and Philadelphia, Pa, Falmer Press.

Whorf, B. L. (1956) *Language, Thought and Reality: Selected Writings of Benjamin Lee Whorf*, ed. J. B. Carroll, Cambridge, Mass., MIT Press.

Wilkinson, A. M. (1965) with contributions by A. Davies and D. Atkinson, *Spoken English*, *Educational Review*, Occasional Publication no. 2, University of Birmingham School of Education.

Wilkinson, A. M. (1968) 'The Implications of Oracy', *Educational Review*, vol. 20, no. 5.

Wilkinson, A. M. (1970) 'The Concept of Oracy', *English Journal*, vol. 59, no. 1.

Wilkinson, A. M. (1971) *The Foundations of Language*, Oxford, Oxford University Press.

Wilkinson, A. M. (1975) *Language and Education*, Oxford, Oxford University Press.

Wilkinson, A. M. (1985) 'Argument as a primary act of mind' paper presented at

International Writing Convention, University of East Anglia. In A. Wilkinson (ed.) (1986) *Aspects of English Composition. Educational Review Special Issue*, vol. 38.

Wilkinson, A. M. (1986a) *The Quality of Writing*, Milton Keynes, Open University Press.

Wilkinson, A. M. (ed.) (1986b) *The Writing of Writing*, Milton Keynes, Open University Press.

Wilkinson, A. M. (1986c) 'Argument as a primary act of mind', *Educational Review*, 38, 2.

Wilkinson, A. M. and Stratta, L. (1969) 'The evaluation of spoken language', *Educational Review*, 21, 3.

Wilkinson, A. M., Stratta, L. and Dudley, P. (1974) *The Quality of Listening*, London, Macmillan.

Wilkinson, A. M., Barnsley, G., Hanna, P. and Swan, M. (1980) *Assessing Language Development*, Oxford, Oxford University Press.

Wills, D. M. (1977) 'The ordinary devoted mother and her blind baby', *The Psychoanalytic Study of the Child*, 34.

Yule, G. (1985) *The Study of Language*, Cambridge, Cambridge University Press.

Name index